ABOUT

Lindsey Agness is the bestselling *with NLP* and an experienced NLP. As MD and founder of The Change Corporation, she works with some of the biggest businesses in the country, as well as running courses and seminars for individuals.

Having been on her own personal midlife journey of change, Lindsey is well-equipped – on both a professional and a personal level – to advise women on how to change their own lives. She now offers one-to-one coaching on this topic, as well as a highly successful programme entitled 'Age with Attitude'.

www.agewithattitude.co.uk
www.thechangecorporation.com

WHAT OTHER WOMEN ARE
SAYING ABOUT LINDSEY

'Lindsey Agness provides you with an opportunity to change the way you live your life and achieve your dreams.'
JANICE FROM HERTFORDSHIRE

'Lindsey has helped me turn my life around. I was living in the Grey Zone and had been for many years without realising it. Lindsey and NLP gave me the tools to put my life back together and be clear on what I want out of life.'
OLIVIA FROM SOMERSET

'You will come away with an amazing set of new skills and life will never be the same again.'
KAY FROM MANCHESTER

'Lindsey Agness is an exceptional and gifted trainer. Her courses and books are daring and empowering – for the woman/women who want to soar in their midlife.'
IRENE FROM LONDON

'My goodness where do I start? Emotionally I've learnt so much. I've grown as a person, as a mother, a friend and a daughter. I have expert tools to help me go out and earn money from my new skills, and I've met a wonderful bunch of new friends.'
JENNIE FROM ASHFORD

'A lot resonated with me from this book and I feel this will focus me in my goals which I haven't, yet, achieved.'
VIVIENNE FROM SUSSEX

Still

25

Inside

8 STEPS TO FEELING HAPPY, HEALTHY AND FULFILLED – WHATEVER YOUR AGE

LINDSEY
AGNESS

RODALE

CANCELLED

This edition first published 2010 by Rodale
an imprint of Pan Macmillan, a division of Macmillan Publishers Limited
Pan Macmillan, 20 New Wharf Road, London N1 9RR
Basingstoke and Oxford
Associated companies throughout the world
www.panmacmillan.com

ISBN 978-1-905744-55-8

1 3 5 7 9 8 6 4 2

A CIP catalogue record for this book is available from the British Library.

Cover design by Stuart Brill and Katie Tooke
Text design by James Collins

Printed and bound in the UK by CPI Mackays, Chatham ME5 8TD

The names of the individuals who appear as case
histories in this book have all been changed.

Mention of specific companies, organizations or authorities in
this book does not imply endorsement by the publisher, nor does
mention of specific companies, organizations or authorities in
the book imply that they endorse the book.

Visit www.panmacmillan.com to read more about all our books
and to buy them. You will also find features, author interviews and
news of any author events, and you can sign up for e-newsletters
so that you're always first to hear about our new releases.

RODALE
LIVE YOUR WHOLE LIFE

We inspire and enable people to improve their lives and the world around them

Contents

This book is dedicated to my father, who
continues to teach me the qualities of courage,
stability, integrity, resilience and dedication.
Thank you. My life is richer for loving you.

INTRODUCTION

Is This It?

Still 25 Inside is a book written for midlife women everywhere – women who believe in beginnings, not endings, and who want the next phase of their lives to be as good, or better, than anything they have experienced so far. In our image- and age-obsessed society it's high time that attention was paid to women in the middle phase of their lives. For the record, 'middle' can mean anything from late 30s through to late 50s, depending upon when things have happened to you. The important point is that if you feel as if you are in this new phase, then you probably are.

We are not the 'invisible generation' and we are far from 'done'. We want to be vibrant and alive, and embrace the changes that we are experiencing as opposed to mourning them. While the media might portray us as 'over the hill', reinforced by the regular sackings of older women from our television screens, this book shows that ageing is an 'Attitude' of mind. You can choose to feel good about yourself and enjoy life, or you can choose to withdraw into the shadows and worry about the ageing process. Which is it to be for you?

So, what is an Attitude? Our Attitudes are made up of what we believe about ourselves and what's important to us. Feeling good and enjoying life is a mindset that all of us can develop. You can make this choice at an emotional level (in terms of how you feel about yourself) and at a psychological level (in the way that you behave). Your chronological age is *only* a number. What really makes the difference is a positive state of mind – living a life that you're passionate about, and having fun. When you achieve these things a magical thing happens. You look and feel good, no matter what the year of your birth. The following chapters will show you how to achieve that for yourself.

For this book, I've developed the '8 Attitudes of the Successful Midlife Woman' to provide you with a practical approach and the necessary tools both to help you work out what you want from your life and to challenge any doubts you might have had about what is possible for you. These Attitudes will give you a new focus and purpose and help to increase the joy and passion in your life. A word of advice, though: before you make any radical changes in your life, such as spending a small fortune on cosmetic surgery, leaving your career or even ending a long-term relationship, read this book first and discover what you want to be, do and have. How do you do this? By adopting the 8 Attitudes of the Successful Midlife Woman. As you take this journey, notice how you automatically begin to change from the inside out, discovering a permanent and deliberate way of thinking and behaving, which delivers long-term results.

I will be your coach, guiding you on every step of your journey. You may be wondering how I can make these rather ambitious claims, and how I am qualified to act as your guide. So, here's a bit about me. During my 40s, I made four life-changing decisions – to leave my marriage, abandon my well-paid corporate consultancy career, start my own business and embark on my first writing project. As a result, I've had to work hard to build a new life for myself and my family, and the last few years have called for some sacrifices. Giving up a large corporate salary means that I have lived on as little as I possibly could over the last four years in order to build my business and look after my family. I even down-sized my house in order to make my income go further. I have worked long hours and made sure that any time spent with my children has been 'quality' time. I have also put the possibility of a new relationship to one side, while my energy and focus has gone into discovering my life's purpose. And, at times, I've struggled to maintain a healthy lifestyle with no one in the background to spur me on.

Yet, now I can pretty much do, be and have what I want in my life. Everything I have achieved I have done by living and breathing the 8 Attitudes of the Successful Midlife Woman. I developed the Attitudes while on my own personal midlife journey of change, and have discovered that they hold the key to what *really* enables women of our generation to make a success of their lives. I mean success in its widest sense – career, relationship, health and fitness, finances, moving on from an empty nest, making new friends, building confidence and self-esteem – whatever success means to you. I'm a trainer of Neuro Linguistic Programming (NLP; see page 265 for a full description of the science behind this discipline) and I've used NLP as the basis of the change technology in this book. NLP was founded on the basis of a question: 'What makes the difference between someone who is world-class at what they do and someone who is mediocre?', so it was a perfect starting point for this book. I've used NLP as the foundation for the 8 Attitudes because I want to move us away from midlife mediocrity towards midlife excellence and success.

Midlife provides a moment of truth for all of us; it is a time when we question what we want to do with the rest of our lives and who we really are. It also provides an opportunity unlike no other, to step outside of the place I call the Grey Zone. The Grey Zone is that comfortable yet uncomfortable place where the majority of the population spend their lives preferring familiarity over fulfilment. The successful midlife woman realises that time speeds up as the years go by, so let's get on with the business of creating what you want in your life.

The good news is that as we approach midlife we've learned valuable lessons from our journey so far. Whatever choices we've made, whether they have been to be a wife, partner, mother, career woman, a carer for parents or to live alone, we have learned a great deal about what is really important to us. We can use those experiences now to assist us in creating our future. What is so thrilling about *now* is that you know in your heart that the next phase of your life has the potential to be more exciting than anything you have experienced so far. That's why you picked up this book! You're just not sure yet how to get started, and that is where I come in.

As you read this book, I want to invite you to suspend your beliefs and judgements about what is possible for you, so that together we can become explorers in a world where boundless energy, beauty, happiness, worthiness, creativity and fulfilment are common experiences in our everyday lives. People want to be around us, to share our universe because we have something wonderful to contribute. We are admired and we enjoy our lives. This period of our lives is our best. It is our best because we have the opportunity to discover who we are and to share our knowledge and experiences with others. We have the opportunity to use more of our time for us and to explore all those things we have always wanted to do.

A recent study called 'The Paradox of Declining Female Happiness' has provoked a storm by suggesting that while men have become more satisfied with their lives since the early 70s, women have become more miserable. Our lives have undoubtedly become more complex and we simply have too much on our plates. I am absolutely not, however, suggesting a return to the kitchen. Living the 8 Attitudes of the Successful Midlife Woman brings more joy, purpose and balance into our own lives, and also helps us set a healthy example for our daughters. We begin to draw new boundaries for ourselves and use our time differently.

What you may be experiencing now is definitely *not* 'it'. So, are you ready to have the time of your *mid*life?

Take a long, hard look at yourself

As a business consultant, I learned early on that it is important to be able to measure our success, or, in the context of this book, the level of satisfaction we feel about who we are. With that in mind, I want you to take a long, hard look at yourself. When they reach their 40s and 50s, many women ask themselves questions about what they have achieved so far (and what they haven't), where they are going and what they would like to change. Marriage, partner and career often no longer hold the appeal that they once did. You look in the mirror and you wonder who is looking back at you.

Are you a mother who started your family at a young age and now find that your children have flown the nest and you have too much time on your hands? You may be feeling lost and empty. Or perhaps you are a mother who started a family at a much later age and now find that you are consumed by children at a time when your friends are having fun? You may be feeling frustrated with life. Maybe the things that have consumed you over the past 20 years, such as cooking, shopping, chauffeuring and entertaining, are no longer required? Or are you a woman who looks at your partner of many years, and realises just how miserable and lonely you are in a relationship that has become dull and routine? You may be feeling trapped in your life. Are you the career woman who has spent many years breaking through the glass ceiling only to find that corporate success holds none of the appeal that was once promised? You may be feeling you've sacrificed too much.

Or maybe you have dedicated your time to being a carer and now wonder where the years have gone? You may be feeling tired and alone. Do you notice yourself avoiding the mirrors in your house, and wondering where that Twiggy-like body went? You may be feeling disappointed with yourself. Or perhaps you just want to hold on to that amazing life that you already have and are anxious about the impact that growing older might have on it. Whatever your situation right now, be honest with yourself. The important thing to realise is that life begins to change from the moment we make a decision to do something different.

To find out exactly where you are now, take the quiz opposite. Your answers will also act as a benchmark for measuring your progress as you journey through this book.

● EXERCISE I
What's age got to do with it?

1. How much 'me time' do you take per week, on average?
a. More than 5 hours per week
b. Between 1 and 4 hours per week
c. None

2. When was the last time you had exciting and passionate sex?
a. This week
b. In the last 6 months
c. Can't remember!

3. Last time you looked at your partner did you:
a. Feel blissfully in love
b. Wonder what happened?
c. Feel completely trapped

4. Would you consider cosmetic surgery?
a. No, I don't need it
b. Maybe
c. Definitely, if I could afford it

5. When you look in the mirror do you:
a. Feel happy with what you see
b. Know there's some work to be done
c. Ban all mirrors in the house!

6. How often do you exercise?

a. More than once a week

b. A couple of times a month

c. Never

7. Do you have goals for the future that stretch you?

a. Yes, I'm very focused

b. I have a few

c. I don't have any goals

8. Are you on track with your career?

a. Absolutely

b. Used to be

c. I've given up and am coasting to retirement

9. Is your work aligned with your core talents?

a. Yes, I love my work

b. Not really, but it pays the bills

c. No, my talents are totally wasted

10. Are you continually competing with younger women at work?

a. Yes, and I win!

b. Sometimes

c. All the time

11. How do you feel most of the time?

a. Energised and happy

b. Could be better

c. Pretty depressed

12. Do you believe that the best is yet to come?

a. Of course

b. Convince me

c. You must be kidding …

Now, add up the number of As, Bs and Cs, and find out what your choices suggest about you:

MOSTLY As: Congratulations! You are well on the way to breaking through to a new you, and I'll show you how your life can get even better.

MOSTLY Bs: Your life doesn't matter enough right now, does it? You are probably feeling pretty stuck and unfulfilled. It's time to work out what you really want to do with the rest of your life. I'll help you develop some ideas to do just that.

MOSTLY Cs: You've really bought into the media hype, haven't you? You believe it's too late to change. Be brave and dare to explore the possibilities of something different. I'll show you how.

Midlife women are achieving more

These days, there are certainly more midlife role models, and women of our age are achieving more. If 50 is the new 40 and 40 the new 30, then the opportunities open to us are far greater than those offered to our mothers and grandmothers. There is far more out there for women of our age if we choose to seek it out. Whether you love them or hate them, these are some of my favourite female icons who have helped move the image of older women forwards in the last few years. Dame Helen Mirren, born in July 1945, has won an academy award, four SAG (Screen Actors Guild) awards, four BAFTAs, three golden globes and four Emmy awards during her illustrious career. A few days away from her 63rd birthday she was caught by the paparazzi wearing a red bikini on holiday in Italy with enviable curves and a flat stomach. Twiggy, born in September 1949, has been the face of Marks & Spencer since 2005, a successful author herself, and still an icon of style and fashion in her late 50s and early 60s. J. K. Rowling, born in July 1965 and author of the Harry Potter books, progressed from living on welfare to multi-millionaire status within 5 years. In 2008, she was cited as the 12th richest woman in the UK by *The Times*. A truly inspiring story.

On the other side of the Atlantic, Michelle Obama, born in January 1964, was thrust onto the world stage at the time of her husband's election campaign. Her charisma and warmth even encouraged the Queen of England to make a public display of affection by slipping her arm around Michelle – the first time the monarch had ever been seen to make such a gesture to someone she had only just met. Condoleezza Rice, born in November 1954, was the first African-American female Secretary of State with the George Bush administration. Madonna, who turned 50 in 2008, demonstrates how working out can keep your body in shape and give you the energy to achieve whatever you want. Between July and August 2009 she starred in 30 concerts on her Sticky & Sweet Tour. That's one concert every other night, which is both physically and mentally exhausting. And, Oprah Winfrey, talk-show host and author, born in January 1954, is ranked as the wealthiest African American of the 20th century and the greatest black philanthropist in American history.

All these women have something in common – they have passion and authenticity, and they inspire us to find another way through our midlife. I wonder which female icons are your personal favourites? Who inspires you to do something different? List them below along with the reason why you have chosen them.

● **EXERCISE 2**
My favourite female icons

List their names and the reason why you have selected them:

Name ....

Why chosen ....

....

➤

Name ....

Why chosen ....

....

Name ....

Why chosen ....

....

Celebrate your successes

If midlife female icons are achieving more in their lives, let's also remember what you have achieved so far in your own life, and the value of those experiences. Of course, you don't have to be an actress, supermodel, famous writer or entrepreneur to have led a successful life. We will all have done things we are proud of, and midlife is a time to be grateful for everything that we have achieved so far. In fact, the beautiful and glamorous Julianne Moore (48) recently said in *Vogue*: 'The great thing about middle age is that you at least reach the point where you can go "I like it here".'

This is an excellent moment to remind ourselves of our successes in life, and what we have to be grateful for. There are always lots of things to include, even if the list might seem a little sparse at first. That's because at a very young age we are often taught to focus on the things that we do 'wrong', or that don't go to plan. It's almost as if we wear a pair of sunglasses that filter out all of our positive experiences.

For now, though, let's explore your biggest achievements to date – those things that you are most proud of. These might be anything from raising a family and running a home, to being successful at work, learning something new or getting fit. Think over all areas of your life. I know you'll be surprised at what you come up with.

If you cannot think of at least 10 things, then ask your family and friends. I'm sure they will come up with some more with you.

● **EXERCISE 3**

My greatest achievements so far ...

First of all, list below the things you have achieved in your life so far. Choose the ones that provoke the greatest feeling or emotion. Aim for a minimum of 10!

1. ....
2. ....
3. ....
4. ....
5. ....
6. ....
7. ....
8. ....
9. ....
10. ....

➤

Next, I want you to transfer this list onto a large piece of paper and place it where you can see it every day. You may also want to transfer it onto a smaller piece of paper and carry it with you in your handbag, so that every day you can remind yourself of all the things you have achieved. As you look at the list, remind yourself that these are the things you can be grateful for in your life. This will begin to shift any negative feelings you have about yourself and help you begin to develop greater levels of self-confidence and self-esteem.

Finally, I want you to ask yourself what you have learned from each of these valuable experiences. For example, if you wrote down bringing up children, ask yourself what that has taught you. When I think of my own amazing children, I believe that I've learned to teach, give unconditional love, find happiness in the simple things in life, provide discipline, motivate and coach, be proud and have hope for the future. When I think about setting up my company, I believe I've learned to become an entrepreneur, to take risks, to be creative and to give others more choices about how they live their lives. I feel good as I reflect on my contributions so far. Now it's your turn.

1. ....

2. ....

3. ....

4. ....

➤

5. ....

6. ....

7. ....

8. ....

9. ....

10. ....

These experiences are what will give you the confidence you need to make your future everything you want it to be. Instead of the rest of the world believing we are invisible, now is the time for us to have the courage to empower ourselves and be noticed. Have you ever wondered why we experience menopause at midlife? My personal theory is that it's our time after childbearing years are over to be free to' make the changes we want to make in our lives It's your time to come on board, so take the opportunity right now to take that first step.

Midlife: The age of liberation

Our personal values alter as we grow older. Those things that seemed important to us in our 20s and 30s no longer hold the same appeal. We want to do more for ourselves and with our lives. Dr Pam Spurr, writing for the *Daily Mail* in March 2009, says that 50 is a 'dangerous age for women – and it's become so increasingly over the past years – because they now feel they want and need more from life than what they have.'

This might explain why the divorce rate is soaring for women of our age. Surprisingly enough, a new survey in the US shows that it's women who instigate the divorce proceedings in 65 per cent of cases.

There's something that happens to the way you think and feel when you turn 40 and I personally found that it's even stronger when you turn 50. I had my 50th birthday last year, and I was absolutely dreading it. In fact, I wasn't going to celebrate it in any way. Then one of my best girlfriends challenged me by asking who was I to prevent my friends and family from celebrating with me! That was a good reframe. So I decided to go ahead and have a party and it turned out to be a fabulous evening. Even more amazing was the shift I experienced in myself over the period around my birthday. It felt like a heavy load had been lifted from my shoulders. Not only because I had finally come out of the 'closet' about my age, but also because I realised that I just didn't give a stuff any more about pretending to be anyone other than who I really am. That felt incredibly liberating. It may have been the seismic hormonal shift I've been experiencing recently (brought on by the menopause), or it may just have been the fact that I'm finally learning to be myself. Hallelujah!

I was surprised and delighted recently when I read that Michelle Pfeiffer spoke of turning 50 in an almost identical way to me: 'Surprisingly it has left me feeling liberated in a strange kind of way. Sort of, the pressure's off. And it's actually quite wonderful. I wasn't expecting that.'

Your midlife is a time to step back and evaluate what truly makes you happy – and what doesn't. This is a time for you finally to experience the freedom to be who you want to be and achieve everything you set your mind to. Whichever aspects of your life you want to make a difference to, midlife is certainly a time for reflection and change.

● CASE HISTORY: **SONIA**

Living the dream

Sonia is in her late 40s and had been married for 25 years. She is a successful businesswoman, who would fit well in any executive team. Her husband had been one of her first lovers and they lived in suburbia with their teenage son, who is 13. An opportunity arose for Sonia to travel to Tunisia, and it was the first time she had holidayed alone. She wanted some quiet time to herself, so it took her completely by surprise when she met a handsome young Tunisian man. They had a brief holiday romance. She realised that she had felt truly alive for the first time in years, and when she returned home, it caused her to begin to question the state of her marriage. She began to notice things that hadn't bothered her before. Her husband was a few years older than her and had begun to act like her father as opposed to her lover. He was asleep in the armchair by 9pm each evening and moaned about everything. She couldn't remember the last time he had taken her out for a nice romantic meal or when they had spent quality time together. She worked hard over a period of two years to make changes in the relationship, including being very open with her husband about her feelings, going to Relate, and having other coaching. Her husband didn't

➤

take her seriously at first. Sadly, despite her best efforts, the marriage failed and Sonia found herself living alone for the first time in many years.

Sonia decided to travel to Tunisia again. This time, it felt wildly exciting to be travelling as a single woman and doing something different. On her very first night she met a younger Tunisian man in the bar of her hotel and they chatted until the early hours. During the week they became inseparable, and though her friends looking on may have questioned whether this was a Shirley Valentine moment, Sonia and the handsome Tunisian became lovers. His dark skin and youthful body awakened something in her that had been dormant for many years. When she returned to the UK she felt liberated and beautiful for the first time in a very long time. Her friends noticed a sparkle in her eyes that had been missing, and also how she began to pay much more attention to her appearance. And, the story doesn't end there because Sonia has been back to Tunisia several times, proving that there is love after Shirley Valentine! She is deliriously happy and whatever happens in her new relationship she will never be the same again. In fact, she's now considering starting a new and simpler life in Tunisia when she retires.

Of course, this total shift of lifestyle does not happen to us all; yet, to a greater or lesser extent, we will experience our values changing during this period. Warn your family and friends now!

The age with attitude model

My inspiration for this book came from an exhibition that I went to recently, which focused on 50-year-old women. I booked a stand at the exhibition and I also signed up to give a talk about how to change your life at 50. My team was very excited about visiting a new exhibition to learn more about this age group. What I found was not what I had expected. I was astonished to see that on the exhibition promotion website were adverts, not from companies promoting vitality, self-esteem and confidence, but for cancer relief (as it's inevitable we'll be one of the millions catching this disease, won't we?), laser treatment for eyesight (because we all know your eye sight starts to fail after the age of 45, don't we?), how to sleep better without any aches and pains (because we all know that you can't sleep as well as you get older, can you?) and the best of all – who we will leave our fortunes to when we die (because it's not far off now, is it?). Coming away from the website, I felt like the end of my life was nigh and that I'd better make some plans for my demise ... fast! I started to feel rather uneasy about the whole thing. However, we'd booked already and so off we went one bright and sunny September morning. My uneasiness was reinforced once we arrived, because instead of being surrounded by exhibition stands promoting the hugely positive aspects of being 50, we were surrounded by stair lifts, pension plans, retirement villages and ballroom dancing. Even the keynote speakers were talking on the dynamic topics of cooking and gardening.

Needless to say, not many women our age could be seen at the exhibition – most were 70-plus! Could that be because most of us feel that there's still lots of life in us yet, and more to aim for than cooking a nice meal for the family or planting a few peonies?! This experience really inspired me to challenge what I began to call the 'midlife myths' and the way people perceive this important time of our lives. The myths are those commonly held views of midlife women found in the media, on our TV screens and elsewhere (such as at that exhibition). We are brainwashed into believing them to be true and representative of our own lives. As a result of this, we become our own worst enemies when we begin to think about what might be possible for us. Do men have a similar challenge, I wonder? Or is it, as I suspect, just we women who are persuaded to feel this way by the society in which we live? We begin to limit ourselves because of what we absorb through the media. We allow ourselves to take on the limiting beliefs that are pervading our lives. But, our lives do not have to fall into this inevitable decline. We're not dead yet!

I've created the '8 Attitudes of The Successful Midlife Woman' as a direct challenge to these myths. When applied together, these 8 Attitudes create the necessary mindset for all midlife women to live their lives with purpose, passion and fun. The attitude we have towards a subject is formed as a result of both our values and our beliefs. Our values represent what is most important to us and they are what motivate us to take action. Our beliefs about ourselves are what determine our confidence levels and self-esteem, which in turn determine whether we feel we can achieve what we want. They work like an on/off switch. For example, if I don't believe I'm capable of learning to dance, chances are that I won't be able to do it, or I will sabotage myself in some way. In the context of this book, each Attitude represents a way to enhance your values and beliefs about midlife in such a way that your spirit will be revived. When you adopt these

8 Attitudes you will achieve the results you want in your life – and you will believe you can and deserve to do so. I promise you that these Attitudes can, and will, change your life!

This book is divided into 8 main chapters, each teaching you the tools and techniques required for you to be able to embrace and adopt each Attitude. Along the way, you'll also find exercises to complete, which will alter your beliefs about what, and how much, you can achieve. Once you reach the last page and complete the final exercise, my aim is for you to possess a completely new way of thinking that will change the way you view life once and for all.

Midlife model of change

These are the most common myths I have come across in my research and in my coaching of midlife women. How many of these myths have you noticed yourself thinking, feeling or even saying out loud?

MYTH: I'm too old to have what I want.
SYMPTOMS: You feel like you are just going through the motions and your days lack vision, focus and goals. You are scared of the emptiness that haunts you and terrified to admit it to anyone else. You have little to excite you in your life.
ATTITUDE 1: 'I live my life on purpose.' You'll regain your sense of self, passion and direction for the future.

MYTH: I've squandered my dreams!
SYMPTOMS: You feel disappointed in yourself and regret the years of procrastination and lack of achievement. You wonder about what might have been. You lack the courage to be, do or have what you really want.

ATTITUDE 2: 'I create what I want'. You take control of your thoughts to focus on what you want and you take responsibility for changing your future.

MYTH: I don't know who I am any more.
SYMPTOMS: After years of focusing on others, you are feeling confused about who you are. You lack confidence and feel that you don't deserve any better. You are easily controlled by others because of your lack of independence and assertiveness.
ATTITUDE 3: 'I know who I am.' You discover who you truly are at your core and stop trying to be something or someone else.

MYTH: It's better to be secure than happy.
Symptoms: You would rather maintain the status quo than risk doing something different. You feel frustrated with yourself because you are dependent on someone or something, and you avoid going for what you really want. There is a lack of honesty in your life.
ATTITUDE 4: 'I am true to myself.' You absolutely know what you want; you respect yourself and you are prepared to disappoint others to be true to your own dreams.

MYTH: I'm not good enough to compete with younger models.
SYMPTOMS: Maybe you have lost out to a younger woman recently in your career, relationship, sport or another area of your life. You feel invisible, lack self-esteem and do not believe in your own attractiveness. This leads to resentment and self-loathing. There is a lack of self-love in your life.

ATTITUDE 5: 'I am good enough.' You have the confidence and self-belief to succeed in whatever you set your mind to, and you believe that you can hold your own with anyone.

MYTH: I need surgery to feel good about myself.
SYMPTOMS: You are likely to have an ongoing fight with food and a low self-image of yourself. This leads to a lack of discipline relating to food and exercise, as well as low self-confidence and a belief that cosmetic change will make you feel better about yourself.
ATTITUDE 6: 'I like myself.' You take control of your lifestyle, from health and fitness to midlife sex, which enables you to feel and look great from the inside out.

MYTH: I don't have enough time or money to change.
SYMPTOMS: You are apathetic about your life; you make lots of excuses to avoid doing anything different and you give up very easily. You lack energy and morale to do something different with your life.
ATTITUDE 7: 'I take time for me.' You feel that the pressure is off and that you live in the now; you take time for yourself, tackle the issues on your mind and go for it.

MYTH: It's just too late.
SYMPTOMS: You play the ostrich and bury your head in the sand. You are very cynical about life, and about your ability to change. You are not prepared to reassess how you live your life. Your life lacks passion and spontaneity.
ATTITUDE 8: 'I'm certain of my success.' You believe your success is inevitable and you are as certain about your future as you are of your past.

I'm curious to know how many of these resonate with you. Maybe they all do. Be honest with yourself and go back through all the myths and assess how many are currently true for you.

Remember for a moment what it was like to be in your early 20s. Maybe you were at university and the world was at your feet; maybe you were starting out at work and feeling full of excitement and curiosity about the future; or, maybe you were crazy in love and full of hope. Remember a specific time like this. Imagine floating back down into your body at that time. See what you saw, hear what you heard and really get back the feelings of being purposeful, confident and young – with the world at your feet. Turn up the brightness, the sounds and most of all the feelings. Really get those feelings moving around your body. What would it be like to feel that way again – full of anticipation for the future? Though I can't promise to turn back the clock, the good news is that I can guarantee that life can feel like this again, whenever you choose. We will work together to embed these 8 Attitudes in you, so that you absolutely believe them to be true. They will create a new mindset that will give you the confidence and self-belief to start to make those changes now.

Are you ready to begin?

The myths of midlife women are generalisations. They do not have to be your truth. Be different from the majority of the female population and start to age with attitude!

ATTITUDE 1

I Live My Life on Purpose

Do you remember a time in the past when you were totally focused, with goals that really excited you? When you knew exactly what you were going for and no one was going to stop you? Maybe you were working on a really important project at work or determined to assist your child through their exams, or even had your future partner in your sights? Allow yourself to go back to that time now. Remember that sense of determination and how in control of your life you felt. Wasn't that a wonderful feeling? Well, this Attitude is all about making those feelings a permanent fixture in your life and enabling you to live your life on purpose (in other words, as if you *really* mean it!) from this point onwards.

It's important for each of us to have goals, but we often forget or fail to put aside the time to set them. If you do have goals, that's great – because this Attitude will show you how to become more consistent in achieving them. This is the point at which you need to think about what you would like to change about your life. It could be that you would like to travel to far-flung shores, learn a new sport, language or skill, meet new friends, volunteer, start up a website or a book club, or anything else you set your mind to. Or it could be something more drastic, like changing your relationship, career or where you live. And, don't worry if you're not sure about your goals. This Attitude will help you to focus on what you would like to achieve, and show you how to identify what you really want to change in your life. The first Attitude, 'I live my life on purpose', is all about giving yourself permission to discover what you want to be, do or have with the rest of your life.

No more excuses

One of my favourite poems, 'The Invitation' by Oriah Mountain Dreamer, begins with the lines:

> It doesn't interest me what you do for a living. I want to know what you ache for, and if you dare to dream of meeting your heart's longing.

> It doesn't interest me how old you are. I want to know if you'll risk looking like a fool, for your dreams, for the adventure of being alive.

I often say to my clients that no one ever died from being foolish. When I'm offered the opportunity to experience something new, I say 'yes'. I always learn from these experiences, even if they don't go quite to plan! One of the things that I've realised over the years is that the most successful people are those who have a direction. In fact, there is plenty of research to suggest that there is a direct link between setting goals and enhanced performance.

You may be a woman who has spent much of your time making excuses for not (yet) achieving what you want from your life. Maybe the kids were still at school or your husband needed you to be at home to run the house. Or maybe you had too many financial responsibilities to change jobs or start your own business. Now all of that is changing. The pressure is lifting, and it's time to reconsider and ask yourself: 'What do I want to do with the rest of my life?'

Why do I need goals?

Time spent working on your goals is time *well* spent. In fact, getting this step right is one of the most important aspects of this book. And yet, getting to 'GO' with your goals can be the hardest part. Experts estimate that only 5 to 10 per cent of people bother to think about their goals on a regular basis, and only 1 to 3 per cent have clear, written goals. I have an idea that if I were to ask you whether or not you have set goals in the past, which you actually went on to achieve, you would immediately say 'yes'. And, if I then asked you if you had set goals that you *didn't* achieve, you'd also say 'yes'.

So, the key question is not only how to set goals, but also how to set goals that you know you will achieve. I want you to believe that your goals are absolutely and inevitably achievable. In this Attitude we will learn why we need goals and how to achieve them. Why should you set yourself goals?

● **Goals provide you with a destination.** Most people in the Grey Zone live their lives aimlessly. They drift along without any clear direction. This can lead to emptiness and frustration. When we set goals, we are provided with a road map *and* a destination. It's rather like having a compass for your mind. Our conscious mind is often called our 'goal-setter', and our unconscious mind our 'goal-getter'. Together they work hard on our behalf by searching out ways to achieve our goals. They are constantly seeking more for us. All we have to do is provide a destination. Without one, our success mechanism lies dormant and drifts or, worse, pursues a destination that someone else chooses on our behalf.

● **Goals help you to concentrate your time and effort.** One of the reasons that people with goals achieve such outstanding results is that they have learned how to focus and concentrate their time, energy and resources on a single objective – even if it is just for a few hours at a time. This type of concentrated power can produce results that are much greater than those achieved through the diffused and unfocused energy most of us use to get through our day.

● **Goals provide motivation, persistence and desire.** Most significant accomplishments require resilience and determination. It is very rare for something important to be accomplished successfully on the very first attempt. If you want to achieve anything significant, it is likely that you will learn from your mistakes as well as your successes. High achievers keep picking themselves up after each fall and continue working steadily towards their targets until they finally reach their goal. The 'why' must be big enough to overcome the 'what'?

● **Goals help you establish priorities.** You will find many forks in the road between where you are now and where you want to be. Instead of just going with the flow and letting the 'current' or other people's interests determine where you end up, you have to decide consciously which way to go. Once you have a direction, other choices can be measured by how far they will assist you in achieving your result. Prioritising gets easier once you have a goal, because your goal acts as a filter, weeding out distractions that do not assist you.

● **Goals take you from where you are to where you want to be.** A well-crafted strategy with an accompanying set of intermediate goals provides a framework to reach far-away targets. One of the best ways to deal with a large or seemingly 'impossible' task is to break it up into a series of intermediate achievable steps and get to work on each piece. As Brian Tracy, well-known Canadian self-help author says: 'By the yard it's hard, but inch by inch it's a cinch!'

● CASE HISTORY: **MARIA**
One putt at a time
Maria's husband had been a keen golfer for years, and, because she wanted to spend more time in the fresh air and improve her fitness, she decided to join him. She felt daunted at the outset – there was so much to learn, and she didn't know where to begin. Fortunately, the golf club was just starting a new ladies' academy to encourage more female members into the club, and so

➤

she signed up. Her first few lessons were a nightmare as she tried to remember how to stand and grip the golf club correctly, where to put the 'tee', and how to hit the ball and comply with the rules of the clubhouse. She only seemed to do well at making rather large rivets in the ground! She almost gave up after a few visits, and her head felt like it was about to explode. Taking pity on her plight, Maria's husband treated her to a few private lessons with the golf pro at the club. The pro regularly used NLP techniques to coach his students. At her first lesson, he spent the entire half an hour showing her how to stand and hold the club. She didn't even hit a golf ball! Throughout the second lesson she practised her golf swing. This time she did hit the ball. During the third lesson she focused on the feel of the club on the ball when she hit it correctly. Gradually, she noticed that building up her skill bit by bit was helping her to integrate each additional piece of knowledge, which she was then able to retain and use more readily. After six lessons she was allowed out on the main course and the real fun started! Now she plays regularly with her husband and is in the ladies team at the club.

Maria's story is an excellent example of how you can break down a big goal (i.e., learning to become a proficient golfer), into smaller manageable chunks. Any goal can be broken down into small enough parts to make that first step feel much more do-able and achievable. You then build confidence to move forwards – and apace!

What happens when I don't set goals?

The interesting question is that if goal-setting is such a powerful tool, why don't more people use it?

● **They don't have a good reason to set goals.** You have to be clear about what you really want before you can use goals to help you get it. This chapter will help you to get that clarity about what you want to change in your life.

● **They don't know about the power of goal-setting.** Another reason people don't set goals is that they don't realise the value of goal-setting as a tool for success and high achievement. Maybe they were never introduced to the concept of goal-setting. After all, it is not something usually taught in our school system. If you don't know about a tool, you can't use it. You, however, do know about it, so no more excuses!

● **They don't know how to use it.** Many people think they have goals, but what they really have are just wishes. You ask them what their goals are and they say something vague and generic like 'I want to be rich', 'I want a better job' or 'I want to be healthy'. While these are goals, they are too vague ever to be successfully achieved. The reason for this is that they simply do not spell out exactly what *is* to be achieved. For example, how rich is rich? Is it having £10,000 or £100,000 in the bank? It may also mean rich in something other than money. Goals should be clear statements of intent, not just vague wishes. For example, 'I want to lose 7kg in the next 8 weeks' is a clear and measurable goal. People almost never write down their goals or prepare a plan for achieving them. I'm going to show you how to get started with your own 'Vision Board' and then make a plan for action. We will then get started in Exercise 5: 'The journey begins'.

- **They feel too busy and disorganised.** A common excuse for people not setting goals is that they are too busy and disorganised even to consider taking on new challenges. They reject the notion at a subconscious level and come up with excuse after excuse about why they can't set goals right now. They just can't motivate themselves into believing that they will be able to achieve their goals when they already feel stressed and overwhelmed just trying to cope with their current demands.

- **They become overwhelmed.** Many people are inspired to try goal-setting because they read about it or hear about it on the news. They want to be more successful and achieve better results, and they understand that goal-setting can help them. A large number of them fall into a common trap that quickly leads to stress and frustration, and they often end up abandoning their goals before they even get started. They either have too many goals – which is distracting, and makes it impossible to prioritise – or they have a goal that is so large that they get overwhelmed and do nothing or give up too soon. Think of goal-setting as a muscle. Like any muscle, the more you use it, the stronger it gets, but you have to work at it gradually. Eventually, most people can simultaneously pursue one or two large goals in every important part of their life without feeling overwhelmed. They just have to work at them slowly, to avoid straining their goal-setting 'muscles'. I've advised clients in the past to experiment with a goal-setting notebook that they can use to record and explore ideas. It is also often easier to set short-term and long-term goals if you write them down. The long-term goal is often the 'big' one and the short-term goals are the more manageable steps it takes to get there. For example, my long-term goal might be to run a marathon, but my short-term goals are to build up my stamina and mileage each week over the next six months by starting to run around the block, then my local park, then to the next village, and so on. By doing that I gradually build up the number of times I am able to go out running a week and the mileage I achieve on each run. This is something I can measure, and works as an incentive because I regularly achieve my mini, short-term goals.

What keeps us stuck?

How are you feeling now about setting some goals? Have I convinced you to 'live your life on purpose'? I hope that you're feeling excited. As you think about taking action or moving an area of your life in a new direction, it's normal to feel an uneasiness or fear that rises in the pit of your stomach or some other part of your body. Many women, in particular, feel some trepidation when they begin to consider changing things. We are often very good at creating scenarios in our heads that are far worse than the actual reality of a situation. I bet you've experienced a situation in which you have construed something in your head, only to find that the real thing was far less challenging than you expected. I often ask my clients to think about the worst possible thing that could happen if they go for their goals – in other words, to imagine the worst-case scenario. Because, if you can deal with that, you can cope with anything.

I recently had a client who wanted to leave her job as a social worker and start her own business. When I asked her the question 'What's the worst thing that could happen ...?', she said that she would have to go back to being a social worker. When I reminded her that there was a national shortage of social workers, she understood what I was getting at. She now runs a very successful coaching business.

In order to achieve your goals you should also hang out with supportive people. They will spur you on when you need some additional support. You may even find that you have to distance yourself from those around you who feel threatened by your success. You'll be able to spot them – they are the ones who prefer you as you are and don't want you to change. They're the ones who will find all the potential problems with your ideas. They do this because your action challenges their own complacency.

If you are still fearful of declaring a new purpose in your life, then ask yourself why you are fearful. Maybe you believe you don't deserve the success, or that you are not good enough to achieve it. Beliefs like these can generate a fear of failure or rejection that gets in the way of taking action. We will explore the root of these beliefs and change them when we consider Attitude 5: 'I believe I deserve it'.

I regularly talk about the 'Grid of Life', which is made up of the Brilliant, Grey and Awful Zones. The Brilliant Zone marks the end of our journey – it's the place to which we all aspire, where we have achieved all of our goals. You'll know if you are heading in the direction of the Brilliant Zone because it feels inspirational, risky, developmental and stretching. In my experience, the journey towards the

Brilliant Zone is made up of our best moments when we are as good as we can be and our bodies and/or our minds are stretched to their limit in order to allow us to achieve something special. This is similar to the concept of optimal experience or flow, as described by Mihaly Csikszentmihalyi in his book *Flow*. This book explores how to achieve happiness by transforming boring and meaningless lives into ones that are full of enjoyment.

The Grey Zone is that place where I believe many women spend their entire lives. The Grey Zone isn't awful, but it certainly isn't brilliant either. It's that comfortable yet uncomfortable place where you know you could do better, but you don't even try because it would mean changing something and taking a risk. It's the place where women are prepared to sell out on their dreams for a comfortable existence. What a waste! This might, for example, mean staying in a loveless marriage, sacrificing your needs for others, spending years in a boring job, wanting to travel but not having the courage to go on your own, and so on. Life in the Grey Zone feels familiar, comfortable, unfulfilling and stuck, and those in the Grey Zone do not feel they have any choice but to remain where they are.

The Awful Zone is the place where none of us want to be. If we do find ourselves here, we normally strive to get out as fast as possible. It can feel a depressing place of little hope for or confidence in the future.

So what finally motivates women to move out of the Grey Zone? There are normally two reasons. Firstly, something happens – often a significant negative life event, such as illness, redundancy, bereavement or divorce. 'The straw that broke the camel's back' is a perfectly relevant idiom in this case. Women in this situation slip from the Grey

Zone into the Awful Zone. They get a jolt to their life and suddenly staying stuck is not an option. They finally do something different.

Or alternatively, they have a goal or vision that is so compelling and desirable that they are driven to move out of the Grey Zone. For example, this would include situations such as getting fitter and losing weight, learning a new skill, setting up a business or retraining for a new career.

Personally, I would prefer you to experience the excitement of having an amazing new purpose in your life rather than waiting for a negative experience to finally get you moving. You can make your own choice!

● CASE HISTORY: **NAZMA**

Focusing on her own goals

Nazma is an Indian Muslim living in the UK. She spent much of her early life living in Saudi Arabia where there are very strict limitations placed on the lives of women. In fact, women are still not allowed to drive out there. Back in the UK, her arranged marriage failed and she was left with two sons to bring up with the support of her family. Her family runs a successful business and Nazma works in the business, along with her three brothers and her father. Although the business kept her financially stable, it also kept her firmly in the Grey Zone; in fact, for many years she felt that she couldn't branch out to do anything for herself. Her father and brothers exerted huge pressure on her to stay and

➤

used the financial security as a threat. However, when Nazma reached 40, with her boys at university, she found that she had time to invest in herself. She became a practitioner and then a Master Practitioner of NLP, which opened her eyes to many new possibilities. She realised that above everything else she had to take responsibility for her own life. She began to hatch a plan to escape from the clutches of her well-meaning but possessive family. Being a very focused and determined individual, Nazma had to be patient with her family and chip away at her freedom. Her goal kept her going and small successes have meant a great deal to her. She negotiated working part-time in the family business while going back to art college to pursue her dreams of becoming a designer. She is on her journey out of the Grey Zone for the first time in her life and focusing on what she wants for herself. These small steps have begun to move her towards the Brilliant Zone.

Are we on track?

Before we go any further I want to check that we are on track. How committed are you to making this journey and creating a life to live on purpose? Are you prepared to invest the time required to work out what you want? I'm going to give you one more opportunity to jump ship before the real work begins. So think about it seriously. Are you ready to move out of the Grey Zone, or will you stay stuck where you are forever?

> ● **EXERCISE 4**
> ## Commitment to me
>
> I commit to learning about the 8 Attitudes of the Successful Midlife Woman, beginning right now with Attitude 1: 'I live my life on purpose.' I do this with passion and excitement for the future.
>
> Signed:
>
> ....

The start

Sometimes we wish we had a crystal ball to be able to see into the future. In fact, I'm sure that some of you will have visited a clairvoyant in the past, hoping to find out what the future has in store for you. The risk is that you can put far too much store into what the clairvoyant tells you and then you sit back waiting for your life to unfold as they have described. I prefer to take control of creating what I want and I recommend that you do, too. A few years ago I designed a Christmas card for my clients and I chose a quote for the front that said: 'The only way to discover your future is to create it.' This is the mantra of the woman who chooses to live her life on purpose. We create our future through our goals and the actions we take.

The million dollar question is: *'What do you want?'*

If you're not sure yet, start by asking yourself the following question: 'In which area or areas of my life am I not yet getting the results that I want?'

Key areas of life include career, family & friends, intimate relationships, personal development (such as increasing confidence and self-esteem, learning a new skill, etc.), health and fitness, wealth, and any other area that is important to you right now. Ideally you need to be equally fulfilled in each of these areas in order to achieve harmony, success and the results you want.

● EXERCISE 5
The journey begins

Imagine yourself in three years' time. What do you want to have achieved by then? What will you be seeing, hearing and feeling? Get a really clear image in your mind. Turn up the brightness and size of the image, increase the sounds and ramp up the feelings. Now come back to the present. Using your visualisation, list the area or areas of your life in which you are not yet getting the results you want (for example, health and fitness).

Then, for each area you have identified, ask yourself two questions:

1. What's most important to me about that area?
2. What specifically do I want to achieve?

For question one, you might ask yourself what is important to you about your health and fitness levels. Your answers should reflect what you *want* rather than what you might have now. So you might say: more energy, a nourished body, feeling great — that sort of thing. Get the idea?

For question two, think about what it is you want to achieve. For example, working out three times a week, taking up a new exercise class, losing 20 pounds (about 10kg). It's good to be as clear as you can about these specific goals.

....

....

....

....

....

Once you have identified the areas of life you want to work on, and answered both questions for each area, you are ready to move onto the next stage: developing your Vision Board.

Creating a new map

Now the fun starts. One of the first things I learned as a new practitioner of neurolinguistic programming (NLP) is that our goals need to be more than just words on a piece of paper. The exercises that you have just completed were the warm-up and will have given you lots of ideas about what you want. Now you need to see, hear and feel your goals to be fully associated with and excited about them. In other words, we need to create goals using all of our senses. We do this by creating a Vision Board of what we want.

● EXERCISE 6
My Vision Board

You'll need some materials for this exercise to work best. Search out some colourful women's magazines – magazines that have lots of photographs of interesting people, places and things. Get hold of some felt pens, glue, scissors, a sheet of flip-chart-sized paper and anything else you'd like to use. Now, create some space where you can spread out all your materials.

Think back to the areas of your life in which you want to create better results. Use the magazines to find photographs that represent specific examples of what you want to do differently. For example, if you want to work on your health and fitness, find photos that represent how you want to look and feel at the end of this journey (including your body shape, the clothes you want to wear, your hairstyle, etc.). If you want to work on your career, find photos that represent what you want to do, where you'll do it, the types of people you'll work with, and so on. Or, if you want to work on creating an intimate relationship, find photos that represent what you want from that relationship (including the person, what's important about them, where you want to live, what you want to experience with them and so on). Remember, though, Brad Pitt is spoken for!

Joking aside, when we work on our Vision Board, we find things that *represent* what we want – not the absolutely exact things themselves. For example, you might visualise a man that looks like Brad Pitt, not actually Brad Pitt. That's because wanting a man who is already married or a house that someone else already lives in is unlikely to be right or good for us or for the other people involved. Add quotes and phrases that you find inspirational, as well as any of your own personal images and photos. Do you get the idea? Allow yourself to dream and have fun.

Once you have finished your Vision Board, it is very important not just to look at it but also to imagine the feelings you will experience once your goals are achieved. This part of the process is crucial to its success. So if you have a beautiful new home on your board, conjure up the feeling of what it would be like to live somewhere like that. Walk through your Vision Board house and notice what's in every room. What does it really feel like to live in a house like that?

The next step involves choosing a piece of music that represents your Vision Board. Favourite tracks of mine include 'What Have You Done Today to Make You Feel Proud' by Heather Small, 'Changes' by Will Young and 'No Worries' by Simon Webbe. All of these tracks are about changing your life. Choose your own track that is meaningful to you. Next, think of any tastes and smells that you would associate with your board. For example, one of my clients had a house in France on her Vision Board. Her significant smell was the rosemary she wanted to grow in her new garden; her taste was eating fresh, warm croissants. Another had a trip

➤

to India. Her significant taste and smell were easy as she picked her favourite curry! Choose whatever pops into your mind. You'll be surprised how easy it is for you to come up with these ideas now.

When you have finished your Vision Board, find a way of displaying it so you can see it easily. I buy clip frames from any good art store or somewhere like Habitat or IKEA. These protect your board and make it easy to hang on the wall. At least once a day for two weeks, play your chosen track as you look at your Vision Board. In NLP terms, the two will become neurologically anchored together and after a while you'll find that whenever and wherever you play that music, you will conjure up your Vision Board. Also, imagine the taste and smell of the Vision Board every time you look at it. It makes the whole experience even more powerful.

The secrets of permanent change

Over the years I have learned and experienced a number of finer points about goals that really do make all the difference in the world when you are attempting to instigate permanent changes in your life. I'd like you to take them on board:

- **Let go of the specifics.** I'm now going to say something that may seem contradictory. It's really important to set a path towards your goals. You have done this with your Vision Board. It is then important to take action without mapping out *every single* step of the journey. Why is this? There are a million ways in which you can achieve your goal. If you focus too rigidly on one particular path you will not notice the other possibilities that may come your way. If we focus on just one solution then we miss the opportunity to spot other solutions that may in fact be better ones. Are you with me on this? We end up constraining ourselves and it may take much longer to achieve our goals.

● **Come to terms with the 'secondary gain' of changing.** In the world of psychology and medicine, the term 'secondary gain' is used to define the 'so-called advantages' of staying stuck and not taking any action. I know that the word 'gain' is usually associated with a benefit; however, in NLP terms, it's the benefit of *not* changing. For example, if your problem allows you to miss work, gains you sympathy or financial benefits, these would be examples of secondary gain. These are often an unconscious component of your situation; in most cases you may be unaware of it until someone brings it to your attention. Secondary gain works rather like a set of scales. Until the 'benefits' of changing outweigh the 'benefits' of staying stuck, most people will choose to stay stuck – even if the so-called 'benefits' may seem strange to those of us looking in from the outside. So ask yourself this: if you don't change, what secondary gain might there be for you? If you don't face up to this now, it may prevent you from making the long-term changes you desire. You can discover your secondary gain by asking yourself this question: 'What will I gain or lose by changing?'

● CASE HISTORY: **MIREMBA**

Creating a vision for others

Miremba is Ugandan and has lived in the UK for 20 years, since both of her parents were killed during the Idi Amin regime. She's now in her mid-40s and has built a life for herself and her family in London. I got to know her as her business coach. She had a very strong vision to set up a charity in her homeland, to help women with birth control and protection from AIDS. She wanted to give something back, and this produced a very strong compelling vision for her. We worked together to build her Vision Board, which focused on what the charity would look and sound like, and what it would achieve. Among many other things, it included photos of the women she wanted to assist, a building that symbolised what she wanted to create as her charity centre, and the place where she wanted to operate. She hung her Vision Board in her bedroom so it was the last thing she saw every night and the first thing she saw each morning. Seeing it there every day really inspired her to get started and then to keep going.

She knew that she would have to make some financial sacrifices to set it up and would need to find a way of managing it at a distance, as she couldn't afford to give up her work in the UK to return to Uganda. I'm delighted to say that Miremba set up the charity and it is currently running a programme for young Ugandan women, teaching them about birth control. There are still issues around funding and leadership, yet it's an amazing example of what someone's vision and determination can achieve.

Once you've discovered your secondary gain, you then need to deal with it. As mentioned earlier, it's a good idea to focus on your worst-case scenario. In other words, ask yourself 'What's the worst thing that could happen if I make this change?' Exploring this makes it easier to let go of the secondary gain and move on. This is because the reality of making the change is far less challenging than you probably anticipated. Remember the example of my client, the social worker.

- **Accept that the unconscious mind or our 'goal-getter' does not work in a linear or predictable 'step by step' way.** What this means is that if you set a goal to make, say, £120,000 in a year, you might rationally have worked out that you need to generate £10,000 a month to reach your goal. However, you might find that on the last day of the year you sign a contract for £120,000. That is a rather extreme example and you get the idea. This is important for permanent change because if you do not achieve your goal in the 'rational' way you've planned, you may become despondent and give up. For example, this year one of my goals was to sign contracts with a minimum of six new corporate clients. By April I was still 'off target', from the 'rational' perspective, but I kept focused and kept up all my marketing initiatives. What was interesting was that during that month I signed my six new clients with room for more before the end of the year!

- **Take 100 per cent responsibility for your goals.** I was taught by my NLP teacher that if you are prepared to take 100 per cent responsibility for your goals you

> ## What's your fear?
>
> Fear is the one of the most common reasons why women stay stuck or do not go for their goals. I find this a useful acronym for fear:
>
> **F** alse
>
> **E** vidence
>
> **A** ppearing
>
> **R** eal
>
> If you create a story in your head about the problems of changing, be aware that it is likely to be far worse than the reality. In my experience the reality is often much easier to achieve than you at first believe.

probably won't have to, as your commitment levels, focus and determination will attract people, places and things to you that can assist you. I've personally found that when I've taken 100 per cent responsibility for my choices and actions, I've learned the most, and therefore moved towards my goal that much faster. Have you ever had one of those experiences where you have relied on someone else to do something? Maybe book a holiday or start a new activity? Then they don't get around to it, so you miss out. That's a great example of how you must take 100 per cent responsibility for what you want to create in your life. Of course, the only benefit of not taking full responsibility for your goal is that you will always have someone else to blame.

- **Focus on what you want.** Because we attract to us what we focus on the most, if we focus on not achieving a goal or on losing it once we have it, then we will probably achieve just that. What should you do instead? Always focus on what you want and not on what you *don't* want. Ask yourself what's the worst thing that can happen if you don't get your goal. Notice momentarily that it's not that bad, and then let the thought go. Let me give you an example. A friend of mine set up a very successful training business. I shadowed him in the early days of my business as he had developed a model that totally blew away the competition. I was very shocked when, a few years later, his business went bust. I asked him what had happened and he told me that he realised that he had spent his time worrying about losing the success he had created and then did exactly that. In the next chapter, we'll discover why that happens. For now, however, make sure you don't make the same mistake.

- **Keep going.** I once asked one of my mentors how long I should pursue my goals. His answer was: 'as long as it takes.' In the end, if you follow the recommendations of this book, you will get there. I know because that's exactly what I have done. About a year ago, I decided to go for a new marketing strategy, by advertising one of my personal-development programmes on the radio. I booked 30 seconds of advertising space to be broadcast 34 times in two weeks. It was great fun getting the copy ready and deciding on the script and music. We even had the sound of a hamster in a wheel at the start of the advert, symbolising what it's like to be in the Grey

> The quicker you get opportunities to learn from whatever happens during your journey, the faster you will move forwards. What you learn should always be:
> - **Specifically for you**
> - **Positive**
> - **Future focused**

Zone. I had a schedule of the times that each advert would be playing, and I would listen in excitedly if I was in the office. I even got in additional staff to answer the increase in phone calls I expected once the advert was on air. How many calls do you think we got as a result of that advert? We actually got a big fat zero! That was a great example of when to put something down to experience and move on as quickly as possible.

- **Change your approach.** This is linked to the last point. If you always do what you've always done, you always get what you've always got. If something isn't working, move on. This presupposes that you have a way of getting feedback – and this is very important (see page 29). The feedback from our radio advert was easy to collect. Needless to say, I have not used any radio advertising since my experience. But sometimes it's not so easy and you have to be quite imaginative. Sometimes, if you are personally involved, such as a job or relationship you're not happy with, you will have your own feelings as feedback.

Are you willing to live your life on purpose?

You have worked hard on your goals in this chapter, and you now know that goals are the building blocks of your purpose in life. When you get to Attitude 3: 'I know who I am', you are also going to discover your mission in life. The question now is whether you are willing to risk taking the first step towards your goals.

● EXERCISE 7
What would happen if you did?

First of all, I'd like you to turn the clock forwards 5 years and consider that nothing has changed. You are exactly where you are today. As you think about this, notice that you have a picture in your mind with sounds and feelings attached. What are you doing and saying to yourself? What are others saying to you? What are you feeling? Chances are you are probably experiencing feelings like frustration with yourself and dissatisfaction that you have done nothing. Feel how heavy these feelings are. Now turn them up so they are even stronger and ask yourself, 'When am I going to be prepared to change?'

Clear the screen. OK. I know that probably didn't feel good at all.

Now turn the clock forwards 5 years, having achieved everything that you set out to be, do and have in this chapter. Build a picture in your mind with sounds and feelings attached. What are you doing and saying to yourself? What are others saying to you? As you think about this, notice how much more amazing you feel now. Wouldn't you like to always feel like this?

Clear the screen. OK. I hope that felt completely inspirational.

If you've still got any doubts about your goal, ask yourself the following questions:

- What will happen if I get my goal?
- What won't happen if I get my goal?
- What will happen if I don't get my goal?
- What won't happen if I don't get my goal?

The last of these questions is especially interesting. Your conscious mind cannot process the double negative and so often something pops up from an unconscious level that can guide you to your goal. These questions are good to keep in your mind, whenever you have a challenging choice to make. But, for now, use them simply to realise that you stand to lose so much more from not changing than you do from making your life into what you want it to be.

Feedback is the food of champions

One of the key ways to step up to the next level as quickly as possible is to take action and then get feedback about how you are doing. Feedback often has negative connotations, and it can be as much a positive thing as it can be negative. It is about evaluation, and includes assessing what went well, what needs to be built upon and what could be done better next time. Feedback works when it leads to change. When you take your first steps, it is vital to find a way of measuring your progress. When I described the story of my radio advertising earlier, you could see that the feedback was very measurable – there were no calls. Other times feedback can be more difficult to find; yet it is vital. Feedback can be obtained in many different ways. For example, if you are working on changing your behaviour by becoming more confident or assertive, you can ask friends, family and work colleagues to tell you when they notice a difference in you. If you are planning a new career or relationship, your feedback will be your results in those areas of your life. If you want to make some new friends or take up a new hobby, your feedback is getting out there and doing it and then making note of your results! Here are a few more examples of goals and where the feedback can come from. You'll notice that some are much easier to measure than others.

Goal	Feedback mechanisms
I want to lose 12 pounds (about 5kg)	When I look at my scales they tell me I weigh 12 pounds (5kg) less.
I want to become fitter	My body is toning up when I look in the mirror. I can go for a longer and hillier walk without getting tired or breathless.
I want to visit Australia (or any other country)	I save a little money every week and buy my ticket.

I want to increase my self-esteem	My friends tell me I'm different. I'm experimenting with new activities. I say 'no' more often to the things I don't like. I am more honest and open with my friends.
I want to make new friends	I've been going out more to new places and have made some new friends.
I want a new partner	I make an effort to get out there – going to different places and taking up new activities. I'm meeting new potential partners.
I want to become more confident	I am stretching myself by taking up new hobbies. I am going places by myself now.
I want to learn a new sport	I join the appropriate club and notice that my skills improve, allowing me to play at a higher level/to a higher standard.
I want to improve my job opportunities	I take a development programme and learn something new. I get a promotion.

● EXERCISE 8
Can I give you some feedback?

Now take your goals and work out the ways you are going to get feedback. The examples provided on the previous pages will give you some ideas.

My goals   **How I will get feedback**

1. ....

....

....

2. ....

....

....

3. ....

....

....

4. ....

....

....

5. ....

....

....

➤

Remember that if your actions are not working yet, it's time to do something different. Be prepared to change your approach.

Be gentle on yourself. Each time you take a step forwards while reading this book, give yourself an appropriate treat. Link it to your goal in some way – as long as it's not that muffin you've been missing since you decided to create the body you deserve!

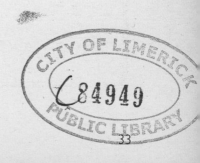

ATTITUDE 2

I Create What
I Want

In this chapter we are going to focus on what really makes the difference between midlife mediocrity and midlife success. We are going to work on change from the inside out. The mind and body are inextricably connected, so when we change on the inside we automatically change on the outside. So often we depend on external 'things' to make us feel better. For example, when we have felt low or unhappy in the past we may have undertaken some 'retail therapy' to make us feel better. However, the feelings of pleasure that this type of thing encourages are normally short-lived. Why? Because we are relying on something 'external' to change the way we feel inside. Because we have tackled the symptom and not the root cause of why we felt bad in the first place. As a result, the effect is always temporary. In contrast, change on the inside is permanent because it's something over which you can take responsibility and control.

Now you have your Vision Board displayed somewhere prominently to inspire you, the next step is deciding how to move forwards. It's time to take some action. This step begins to convince our unconscious mind that we are serious about change, largely because this part of our mind notices things that are different from what it is used to. In other words, our unconscious mind perks up when it senses a little change, and that's the very best way to convince it that we're really serious. And as a result, we begin to attract new people and opportunities into our lives that can in turn bring about more positive change.

I know that it can be difficult to start the ball rolling. The trick is to get started and begin moving forwards as quickly as possible. Unfortunately, this is when many of my clients come to a halt, despite everything else being in place. Why does this happen?

How to stop being a perfectionist

Over the years, I have noticed that many of my clients share the need to be 'perfect' or to take that 'perfect first step', which ends up holding them back. If you demand perfection, tasks simply do not get done on time, or even at all. I used to be a perfectionist myself. I would spend a very long time obsessing over the smallest detail, imagining that someone was looking for my mistakes. To a certain extent, writing has cured me of this, because a manuscript is never totally perfect. Every time you look at it you can find more things to make a little bit better! Before I got into NLP, I used to be very critical of my performance as a speaker and trainer, always focusing on what I had done wrong. Even when I did do something really well I would all too often dismiss it, or pick it apart. I spent lots of my time beating myself up and very little, if any, time congratulating myself.

So where does this need to be perfect come from? It stems from our schooling, parenting, work and, of course, ourselves. We are our own worst enemies, creating unrealistic expectations for ourselves. If someone else can do something to a certain standard then we believe we should, too, even when we haven't had the same experiences, time or training that they have had. We actually set up in our mind the idea that someone is going to judge us. We worry that they will find fault in us, and all our insecurities about ourselves will be revealed. In fact, does anyone really care that much? Sadly, perfectionists live in the future and in the past, worrying about what might or didn't happen. They do not live in the present.

● CASE HISTORY: **SALLY**

Waiting to be perfect

Sally was a student on one of my NLP practitioner-training courses. She is a very rational thinker and likes detail. She's one of those people who believes they need to know 'everything' before they do anything. The trouble is that we never know quite enough … and the more we learn, the more we realise we don't know. It is this mindset that has held back Sally all of her life. She enjoyed the first few days of the training and then began to feel overwhelmed by all of the new knowledge and tools. She was experiencing conflict between her unconscious mind, which was willing her to let go and live in the moment, and her conscious mind, which was desperately hanging on and trying in vain to understand everything that was going on. As change happens at

➤

the unconscious level, this internal conflict inside was preventing her from moving forwards. After the training she went into meltdown, as she compared herself to all the other students and what they were achieving. Even then, she still held herself back, scared of being anything less than perfect.

We worked together and I helped her to understand that being perfect was holding her back from her ideal outcome of being perfect. That double bind really put her conscious mind into a spin. You see, life is not a competition with others or even with ourselves. At any time it's enough for us to do the best with what we know and learn along the way. That's the attitude that moves us forwards fastest. Sally used this advice to begin to relax more and let go of the need for her to know everything before she was willing to take a step forwards. She began to take small risks and experiment with what she had learned on the NLP course with her friends. As that went well, she became more confident to do more and work with others. She's still on her journey and now she's coaching paying clients and living much more in the moment.

Being a perfectionist holds us back from being perfect

We can only become perfect by making mistakes. In NLP we say that 'there is no failure, only feedback'. As a personal development trainer, one of the things that I teach is that mistakes are good. How else can we learn if we don't learn from our errors? We learned to walk by falling over; we learned to balance on a bicycle by falling off, and to ski by falling down, sometimes spectacularly. Making a mistake while trying to achieve excellence and appreciating the mistake for the lesson you get from it is ultimately very rewarding – even if it may not seem so at the time. Accepting that you are likely to make a mistake takes all the pressure off of trying to achieve something – and the irony is that taking the pressure off may actually make it more likely that you will achieve what you are aiming for!

Who sets the standard for perfection? You do. Do you ever achieve it? No, because there is always some minor detail that you could have done better. Perfection is a journey and not a destination. You will always have the opportunity to get it even better next time by learning the lessons from the previous experience.

The first step

So what is that first step going to be for you? Go back to your Vision Board and choose the area of life on which you wish to get started. Maybe you want to develop yourself by building your confidence and self-esteem, start a new hobby, lose weight to get into that stunning summer dress you noticed in your local shop window, or find an amazing new partner. Whatever you choose is perfect. And remember to take the right sized step. How do you know what is right? Well, you should feel stretched and not overwhelmed. It is important to feel stretched so you know that you are doing things differently. In contrast, blind panic is not good for the body! Choose a first step that you know will strike the right balance for you.

● **EXERCISE 9**
Moving in a forward direction

Examples of your first step might be:

- (in the case of business) Go to the next 'women in business' networking event, talk to at least three new people I don't know and come home with at least one important new contact for my business.
- (in the case of health and fitness) Review my diet, cook meals from scratch with fresh ingredients at least three times a week for a period of one month, and review the difference in my weight and energy levels.
- (in the case of relationships) Start a new activity where I know I will meet potential new partners. Talk to at least one person I didn't previously know. Or make sure I go to that next party I am invited to instead of staying at home feeling sorry for myself.
- (in the case of personal development) Read more books, and find out about personal-development taster events (many are free) that I can attend. Target a development programme that I feel will help me the most.
- (in the case of wealth) Pay attention and face up to my financial situation. It's the first step to improving it.

Get the idea? Then, make sure that it is a SMART first step. That means it is:

- **Specific** – you know exactly what you are going to do
- **Measurable** – you know when you have got there
- **Achievable** – it's something that is possible
- **Realistic** – it's stretching you but not giving you panic attacks!
- **Timed** – you set yourself a timescale in which to complete it

The examples opposite are all SMART steps. Make a note of your first step here:

....

....

....

....

....

Once you have committed your first step to paper it is important to build in your mind a picture of what achieving that step will mean for you. Try to create a vibrant picture that will both inspire you and cause you to remember it. Then it's time to start taking action. Keep moving forwards because even if it feels like you're taking two steps forwards and one step back at times, you will know that you are still moving ahead.

You can always make adjustments to your plan if you find that you are not making progress as quickly as you would like. It's also important to praise yourself when you deliver on your first step. I always make a point of treating myself when I've finished something important. For example, book edits are a challenge for me, because once the first draft is written, I want to move on to my next project. So when I complete an edit I reward myself with something symbolic, such as time off, which I use for something like seeing friends, going to the beach or having fun with the kids.

The power of thought

So let me start with the basics first. We alone determine whether our goals will be successful or not. The first thing I would like you to consider is that our reality or the world that we live in can be redefined. In fact, everything can be redefined. Richard Bandler, one of the creators of NLP, once said that it was never too late to have a happy childhood. Our world and what is or isn't possible in it can be redefined because everything that you see around you has been created by *you*. Everything! It is you who are creating your own world, all of it. It is you who are choosing your own thoughts and deciding between what is possible for you to achieve and what isn't. It is you who are bringing people, places and things into being. Without you, literally nothing exists, as it is all in your mind.

You may be thinking that these are all interesting concepts but wondering how are they relevant to you and how you can start seeing some results. Well, I've got good and bad news for you.

The good news is that redefining your world, and therefore your thoughts, is really one of the easiest things you can learn. It is easy because it is something you are already designed to do. It's not an alien concept that you have to struggle to learn. And if you are willing you can learn it any time you want – like now.

And the bad news is that since you were born you have been developing beliefs or 'thought programmes' about yourself that either support you in what you do or in some way hold you back. These beliefs or programmes will be largely unconscious to you; in other words, you may not even be aware of them. Yet, they prevent you from creating your world and your thoughts in the way you want to right now. For example, if you want to learn to play tennis to meet new people, but at an unconscious level you believe you are clumsy, you will either take a while before you get round to signing up, or you may never even try. Or perhaps you want to change your job, but at an unconscious level you believe you're not good enough, so you may well end up sabotaging yourself without even realising you're doing so. In Attitude 5: 'I am good enough', we will learn how to change any limiting beliefs we hold about ourselves. It requires a substantial amount of personal effort and commitment finally to 'wake up' and apply this realisation.

How we create our thoughts

Have you ever been to an event with a friend and wondered afterwards if the two of you actually went to the same thing, as you both interpreted it so differently? Imagine a couple going to the doctor to get a diagnosis for a serious illness that is suspected to be cancer. The diagnosis is confirmed. The person with the illness remains positive and is determined to do whatever it takes to beat the illness. On the other hand, his or her partner is totally negative and fears the worst from the start. Which person is right here? In fact, neither and both are – at the same time. Maybe a more interesting question is which view will give that person the best chance of recovery?

How we respond to the information we receive and the thoughts we create as a result of that information are very significant. Mihaly Csikszentmihalyi, author of *Flow: The Psychology of Optimum Experience*, is one of the few people who has analysed the processing power of the brain. In his book, he estimates that our nervous system – through our fives senses of sight, sound, taste, smell and touch – is bombarded by two million bits of data each second of the day. We can only digest approximately 126 bits of that data – or between five and nine manageable chunks each second. We filter out the rest of the data by deleting, distorting and generalising information that we 'don't need'. That's a lot of data to get rid of. No wonder two people remember the same event differently, as the 126 bits of data that you focus on will be different from the 126 bits of data that I focus on. It's as if each of us has a giant sieve in our nervous system and the 126 holes in my sieve are different from yours. Some may overlap and others will be very different. Therefore, when my two million bits of information are sieved through, I focus on different information and have a completely different experience to you. The 126 bits of data then create what we call in NLP our 'internal representations' or, in other words, our thoughts.

What we delete, distort and generalise depends upon the values and beliefs we have accumulated over the years. For example, if I believe that marriage is a commendable insti-

● EXERCISE 10
Anchor that success

However long it takes for you to take your first step, let's make sure that you enjoy and maximise the moment when you know that you have successfully achieved it. In NLP we know that we can use moments when we experience positive states like success, happiness, confidence and motivation, etc., to help us in the future when we feel less than resourceful. It's a bit like storing positive and life-changing moments in a sort of 'bank' so that you can draw on them whenever you need them. We call these positive moments 'resource anchors' because they literally anchor us back to a positive experience in the past. You can use the moment that you achieve your first step as a positive resource anchor for yourself. It works like this:

1. At the moment that you achieve your first step, take a few minutes to focus only on yourself and what you have achieved.
2. Really enjoy the moment by noticing in detail what you are seeing, hearing and feeling.
3. Ramp up all your senses, especially the feelings of success. When your feelings are at their height, anchor the moment by pressing your thumb and forefinger together. All those positive feelings are now 'anchored' to those fingers.
4. Next time you press them together in the same way, you will feel good about yourself and you can

➤

build upon your anchor as more positive events take place. You can do this by pinching those fingers together each time you find yourself in a positive place and enjoying success. Don't blame me if you notice this happening more and more in future!

5. You can then use your anchor when you are feeling stressed out or anxious about a situation. Fire off your anchor just before you enter that situation and notice how much better you immediately feel.

tution, and my friend believes it is a waste of time, we are likely to have a very different experience of another friend's wedding. Why? Because we each filter the event through our different belief systems. Our filters act like a pair of sunglasses, filtering through only those things to which we decide unconsciously to pay attention. For example, if I have a low self-esteem and I believe I'm not good enough, I will filter out all the times I've been successful and only notice the times I haven't. This is very important.

One of the key assumptions in NLP is that 'The map is not the territory'. This phrase was originally developed by Count Alfred Korzybski in his book *Science and Sanity* to explain how the real world (the territory) and our internalised perceptions (the map) are different. He wrote: 'A map is not the territory it represents, but if correct, it has a similar structure to the territory, which accounts for its usefulness.' What this means is that our perception of reality is not reality itself but our own version of it, or our "map".

Our map can be changed because we have literally made

it up in our heads. We do not experience reality directly, since we are always deleting, distorting and generalising the information as it enters our brain. Essentially, there is only what we create inside of us and then project to the outside world. We can never experience the world around us exactly as it is without it first being filtered by our mind.

If we create our own experience of the world, it follows that we have more choice in life than maybe we thought we had. Often I hear my clients saying things like:

● 'He made me so mad.'
● 'She really disappointed me.'
● 'She upset me.'

In fact, if we create our own world, no one can ever 'make' us do anything. We always have a choice about how we feel because we create our feelings from the inside out. If we choose our own feelings, then we can choose to change how we feel. For example, if my colleague does something that I feel angry about, I am choosing to be angry. It may have been an unconscious choice to begin with, but now I'm aware of it, I can begin to change how I feel. In the amazing book *Man's Search for Meaning*, Victor E. Frankl describes how he survived Auschwitz: 'When a man finds that it is his destiny to suffer, he will have to accept his suffering as his task; his single and unique task ... No one can relieve him of his suffering or suffer in his place. His unique opportunity lies in the way in which he bears his burden.'

Frankl survived by knowing that he was always in control of his thoughts, no matter what was occurring on the outside. That is *real* choice. So, next time you feel less than positive, ask yourself: 'How would I like to feel instead?' Then consciously adopt that feeling.

So how do we do this? The solution is already in hand. You have started moving forwards just by becoming more aware of your filters and your thoughts. We will utilise a number of methods to change our thoughts as we go through this book.

● CASE HISTORY: **BONNIE**

Seeing is believing

Bonnie is a dance teacher. She had a tough working-class upbringing in the East End of London. Her parents separated when she was only a baby, and her mother remarried. Bonnie's stepfather was very critical of her achievements, criticising everything she did, and only ever providing negative feedback. Even when she started her own website for her salsa class, her step-father only pointed out the typos on the site and made no reference to all her hard work and innovative ideas. She could do nothing right.

Not surprisingly, she grew up with a belief that she wasn't good enough. She wasn't aware of this consciously, though she did know that she was very hard on herself. It was as if she was wearing a pair of 'not good enough' sunglasses that everything was filtered through. Because of this belief she had about herself, she never noticed the times she did exceptionally well. She only ever focused on things that had gone wrong.

She came to see me because she was finding running her business very hard going, and she was on the verge

➤

of giving up. We explored her past and the feedback she had been given as a child. We worked on her level of self-belief. For a month, I encouraged her to focus only on what had gone well, until the old pattern was broken. Each day she had to write down at least three occasions when she had achieved something good. This could be a something as simple as going to the gym, or a greater achievement, such as developing a new dance class. This simple task opened her to a new, positive way of thinking. She is now much happier in her work. Success comes more easily and she has a much higher level of self-esteem.

Our secret weapon

We already know that goals give us a target to aim for. What many of us may not know is that we have a part of our brain called the 'Reticular Activating System', or RAS. Your RAS plays a vital part in your ability to achieve goals because it acts like a laser beam, focusing on and bringing to your attention people, places and things that can help you get there.

Imagine that you've set yourself a goal to learn French because you're going on holiday to France – or maybe even considering moving there. One day you've got the radio on in the background while you're cooking the evening meal, as you normally do. You don't pay much attention to it. It's on mainly to keep you company. You notice the general background noise, but you don't bother to listen to each individual advert or general DJ chit chat. But then a new advert comes on giving details of a new French course start-ing at your local college. Suddenly your attention is fully focused on the radio. Your RAS is the automatic mechanism inside your brain that brings relevant information to your attention. It works as a filter between your conscious mind and your unconscious mind. It takes instructions from your conscious mind and passes them on to your unconscious. It's rather like an instruction from your conscious mind to your unconscious mind telling it to 'focus on this ...'.

It's your RAS that does the work by paying attention to the thoughts lodged in your unconscious mind. You no longer have to revisit those thoughts in an active, conscious way. You will have done enough to begin to attract the peo-ple, places and things to you that will help you achieve your goal. That's why your conscious mind is often called the 'goal-setter' and your unconscious the 'goal-getter'.

It's worth bearing in mind some interesting points about your RAS, which make it an essential tool for achieving goals. First of all, you can deliberately program this sys-tem by choosing the exact messages you send from your conscious mind. You can do this by focusing on your Vi-sion Board goals. Eighteen months ago, one of my clients wanted to generate more income and create a different life-style for herself. She was working and living modestly in the South of France at the time. Once she had set her goals, she would regularly drive to Monaco on a Sunday morning and sit among the yachts of the very wealthy. While drink-ing her morning coffee, she enjoyed the view and worked to get a vision of her goal in her mind. She would not only see it, but also hear, feel, smell and taste it. She used her environment to support her in the achievement of her goal. And, although she was creating the images consciously, she was giving her RAS an image to pass on to her unconscious mind with a note that said, in effect: 'Work on this for me please'. I'm not sure if she is living her dream in Monaco yet, but I do know that she successfully acquired two important promotions that changed the possibilities for her and her family.

Secondly, your RAS cannot distinguish between 'real events' and 'imagined' reality. In other words, it tends to believe whatever message you give it. Imagine that you need to have a difficult conversation with someone. You can practise having that conversation by visualising it in your mind. This 'pretend' practice will improve your ability to get your point across. Athletes use this technique a lot – rehearsing their sport in their mind before they actually go out and do it. This is effectively what my client was doing by spending her Sundays enjoying the surroundings and experiences of Monaco, as if she actually lived there. It didn't matter that she might have bought only a cup of coffee and a local paper – she was still acting as if she was already there.

When you set your goal you create a very definite image of it in your conscious mind, with pictures, sounds, feelings, tastes and smells. This is why we worked on your Vision Board first. Your RAS will then pass this on to your unconscious mind – which will help you to achieve your goal. It helps us to achieve goals by bringing to our attention all the relevant information that otherwise we might not have even noticed. In a negative way, our RAS will also prevent our goal messages getting through to our unconscious mind if our self-image is not congruent with our goals. What this means is that if we don't believe we can achieve a goal, we will start to sabotage ourselves unconsciously.

One of the things I've noticed from interviewing successful women is that they focus on what they want. They have priorities for their RAS to focus on, which encourages their RAS to present to them people and things that will help them. Often, it's as if by magic that useful opportunities and people are attracted into their lives to help them. Can you remember a situation when you made a decision about something, and suddenly you began to make useful connections to people and things that could assist you? You may have thought of it as a coincidence, but I don't believe in coincidences. What if it was your RAS acting on your instructions to seek out what you needed? For example, when you are considering buying the latest fashion item, have you noticed how you begin to see women wearing something similar *everywhere*? You might have justifiably wondered where they all suddenly appeared from.

Be careful what you wish for

Of course, if you keep thinking that you can't achieve your goal, your unconscious mind will start to believe that too and encourage you *not* to achieve it. And, if you find you are focusing on other things in your life that you don't want, guess what, your RAS will do an excellent job of delivering those to you, too. For example, if all your focus is going on being in debt, don't be surprised if you find your debt increasing – not the other way around. The reason is that if you're looking at a mountain of debt and feeling terrible about it, that's the signal you're putting into the universe. Your RAS is very obedient and tends to give you exactly what you focus on, whether you want it or not. In addition to all this is another very important fact. Our brains cannot process a negative. It deletes the negation encouraging us to do the one thing we shouldn't be doing! Here's some interesting examples. Last year I was running a leadership programme out in San Francisco, at a very smart hotel. I was there for five days in all. Outside the women's bathroom was a beautiful 4-metre-long, pink, silky-smooth marble shelf. There was a big notice above the shelf that said 'Do not sit here'. As the days went by, I noticed that I was becoming increasingly compelled to sit on that shelf. In the end, on the last day, when I thought that no one was looking, I sat quickly on the shelf with almost child-like defiance. It felt good to sit there, if only for a moment. My brain had deleted the 'not' and had focused on the words 'sit here'! And, the other day much nearer to home, I noticed a worrying notice on a sharp bend close to where I live. It showed a picture of a motorcyclist with 'Crash Site' written above. Oh dear … it's only a matter of time until a motorcyclist takes that as an embedded command, at an unconscious level.

So what's going on in all these examples? First of all, the brain cannot process negatives; so, when we are told: 'Don't think of a blue elephant', a blue elephant is exactly what we think of. In that moment we focus on the very thing we *don't* want, making our nervous system very aware of it. That's what will happen with the motorcyclists, too. As they read the words: 'Crash Site', they get an image in their minds of crashing, which will increase the chance that they will crash themselves.

So, it's vital that you focus on what you *want*, not what you don't want. Go back and make sure that your goals are about what you want to achieve, and are not negative in any way. If you have no goals in life, then your RAS has nothing to go for. If you are drifting from one thing to the next with no focus, then your RAS does not have any clear instructions as to what it should seek out for you. I'm sure we all know people who lead chaotic lives, not settling on anything for very long. Maybe you have experienced life like that up till this moment. Now there are no more excuses. Get your RAS working for you, and use the 126 bits of information you gather every second of your life to help you achieve what you want.

● CASE HISTORY: **MY STORY**

Whatever you do, don't hit the tree

I had gone away on a five-day canal-boat holiday with my teenage son, three of his friends and a girlfriend of mine. The holiday was becoming rather stressful, as the kids didn't really want to help out on the boat, especially when it began to rain and there was no cover over the tiller. My friend Nikki and I took it in turns to steer the 18-metre-long boat and to get cold and wet. It was my turn to steer and as I looked ahead along the canal, I noticed a large tree that had buckled over into the river, with some of its branches lying right in the water at the side of the canal. I calculated that there was just about enough space for the boat to get past. The kids were at the front of the boat playing music and Nikki was inside making tea. The weird thing about canal boats is that you steer them in the opposite way to the direction in which you wish to go. I knew this, and yet I still found the boat moving closer and closer to the tree branches. I heard me saying to myself: 'Whatever you do, don't hit the tree'. As we moved closer and closer to the tree, I heard the voice inside my head shouting louder and louder: 'Whatever you do, don't hit the tree!'

➤

Then there was a loud crash and the lower branches of the tree came in through the window of the boat and for the first time in three days the kids actually shut up for a moment! The really interesting thing is that I knew all about 'focusing on what you want', yet this situation was proof that our programming from the past is so entrenched that we still do what we know to be crazy when we are under pressure. I learned a lot from this incident, and I'm still living down the entertainment that I generated – not only for my family and friends but also other boat owners on the canal!

When you focus on something – no matter what it happens to be – you are calling it into existence. It becomes a *self-fulfilling prophecy*. You have a choice right now. Do you want to believe that things just happen and that what happens to you is just the luck of the draw? Or, do you want to believe and know that your life experience is in your own hands and that good can come into your life because of the way you think and what you focus on? No one would ever deliberately attract what they don't want into their lives. It simply comes from a lack of awareness.

Deletions, distortions and generalisations

Earlier, I mentioned our 'primary filters', which distort, delete and generalise information coming into our nervous system. If you remember, this is how we manage the deluge of data that enters our system every second of the day. So how do we actually reduce a potential two million bits of data per second to 126 bits per second? Let's explore each of our primary filters in turn.

Deletions

If I were to ask you right now to think about how it feels to sit on your chair, you will immediately become aware of the feeling of your bottom on the chair and your feet on the floor, although previously you had unconsciously deleted the information as 'useless' from your nervous system.

Now, read the text you see below:

> **Paris in the**
> **the Spring**

Did you say to yourself: 'Paris in the Spring'? If you did, then you didn't notice that the word 'the' is repeated twice. Look again! Your brain does not expect to see the second 'the' there and so it deletes it.

Our ability to delete information is necessary for us to stay sane. Just imagine if you were to try to process two million bits of data per second. Our brains work like a computer. There is only so much memory at a conscious level for us to use – 126 bits of data per second to be precise. Scientists have proved that all our memories are stored at an unconscious level because we would have no processing power for anything else if they were all stored at a conscious level. You know this as most of the time your memories are not in your conscious awareness unless someone asks you a specific question and then the answers 'pops' into your mind. We also know that under hypnosis, when a direct channel of communication to the unconscious mind is achieved, it is possible to recall memories from the past. The interesting question to ask yourself is what you are currently deleting from your awareness that it would be useful to pay attention to? Maybe you are not yet using your RAS to its full potential, or maybe your limiting beliefs about yourself are preventing you from noticing that it is possible for you have what you want in your life now.

Generalisations

We use generalisations to speed up our learning process. For example, as I walk up to a door handle, I don't have to think about how to open that door. I've opened literally thousands of doors before, and so I can generalise what to do unconsciously, without thinking about it and unnecessarily using up valuable processing power in my brain.

One of the useful things about NLP is that it challenges the generalisations we make and encourages us to take each situation on its own merits. For example, if I hear someone saying: 'I'll never have what I want', I would challenge their use of the word 'never', as it is a generalisation. This is an example of a limiting belief that someone holds about themselves. Beliefs are shaped by generalisations; for example, something happens once and we take it to be true for all other occurrences. Let's say you have experienced a recent redundancy. You might now be fearful that it will happen again in your next job. However, there is no evidence for this – you have just generalised one experience to be relevant to all experiences. The disturbing thing is that in your next job you may start behaving as if redundancy is likely. You might not be as committed or show initiative. The worrying thing is that if any redundancies are required you may well have got yourself to the top of the list. Remember: you get what you focus on! Listen to yourself. Do you use phrases like ' I never ...' or 'I always ...'? These are examples of the generalisations you may use.

Distortions

We make up meanings about things and people all the time. The problem is that these 'meanings' then become our reality, even if they are not necessarily true. For example, if my friend walks straight past me in the supermarket, I might decide that I've done something to upset her. In reality, she may have just been very rushed and didn't notice me. This is important, as we distort events many times each day – and end up distorting reality. We attach meanings that don't exist and often end up making huge assumptions. If we attach the wrong meaning to important issues, distortions can get in the way of our goals. If you're not sure about something or someone, check it out by asking. This is when feedback becomes very useful, and it can encourage open and honest two-way communication between people.

As I mentioned earlier in this section, your thought programming is unconscious and is likely to need some re-design in certain areas of your life – particularly those areas where you are not yet getting the results that you want. In Attitude 5: 'I am good enough', we will work through some tools to assist you. The really good news is that because our perceptions are not real, they can be changed.

A chain reaction

Earlier we explored how important it is to focus on what you want, rather than what you *don't* want. In the canal-boat story, I had filtered out the word 'don't' from 'don't hit the tree', leaving me to focus on 'hit the tree'. And look what happened next! Our thoughts start a chain reaction in our nervous system that it's important for us to explore.

In NLP-speak, the information that we unconsciously filter into our nervous system, via all of our senses, forms our thoughts or internal representations. Our thoughts are made up of a combination of our senses (in other words, pictures, sounds, feelings, tastes and smells). We each have a sensory preference in terms of how we view the world. What do you believe your preference to be? For example, if you see pictures as you think, you probably have a visual preference. If you experience strong feelings as you think, you probably have a kinaesthetic or 'feelings' preference, and so on.

What's important is that the type of thoughts we have will drive how we feel – or our emotional state. If you think back to a time when you were very successful, I'm sure it occurred when you were in a very positive emotional state or mood. You are unlikely to have been depressed, miserable or anxious. So, our results are dependent on our mood or state.

What happens next is that our mental state drives our physiology or body language, our physiology drives our behaviour, and our behaviour ultimately drives our results. So, it follows that our thoughts will drive our results – hence, thoughts become things. As Henry Ford once said: 'Think you can, think you can't; either way, you'll be right.'

Let's explore an example of this chain reaction. Imagine you need to have a challenging conversation with someone. That is the external event. If you have had a number of unsuccessful conversations with that person in the past, you are likely to be filtering that imminent conversation in a negative way. That is to say that you expect the conversation to go badly so, in your head, you begin to tell yourself a story about the conversation going badly. Your thoughts are then focused on the conversation going badly. In turn, that will affect how you feel – and your mood or state. You are likely to feel nervous, uncomfortable and any other variety of negative emotions. And because the mind and body are interconnected, this then impacts your physiology. When you go to have the conversation, the 'receiver' will notice your nervousness. For example, they might spot you fidgeting. Your behaviour is then compromised because you are nervous, and the other person picks up your anxiety and plays on it. The final outcome is that you did not get the result you wanted. Hence, a self-fulfilling prophecy.

The opposite is also true. Let's take the same situation. You have a challenging conversation coming up. This time you remind yourself of the times when you have had successful conversations with this person, which have led to a great result from your actions. This time you are looking forward to the meeting, as you are very confident of your success. You tell yourself a success story and maybe even imagine how you will be feeling at the end of the successful conversation. You are feeling confident and full of anticipation. This time your physiology is different – your posture is much more positive (i.e., you are standing tall, grounded, open and smiling). Your 'receiver' notices how positive you are feeling and responds. You are able to get your point of view across successfully and make some new agreements. You get the result you wanted.

The same external situation had completely different outcomes, each of which was entirely dependent upon how you filter the event from the inside.

● EXERCISE 11
What are you thinking about?

Take a few moments now to let your mind relax a little. Just as we can be aware of our feelings and movements in our body, we can also step back from our thoughts and simply observe them. One thought drifts in, which leads to another and then another until we become lost in our own world. What I want you to do is to simply observe your thoughts as they come and go. Sit still and wait for a thought to arise without attaching any meaning to it. Just observe them coming and going.

For the next day, pay attention to your thoughts and feelings. Notice if your thoughts are positive and supportive to you, or if they are negative and may possibly be sabotaging your chances of success. Make a note of the recurring patterns below, both positive and negative. You may be surprised by the results. Which side of the scales is the heaviest? If it's your negative thoughts, then you have a huge opportunity right now to start changing your thoughts from the inside out.

Positive thoughts and feelings	Negative thoughts and feelings
....	....
....	....
....	....
....	....
....	....

How do I change my thoughts?

There are many ways to reframe our thoughts and we are going to explore a number of methods in this book, starting with the 'Beliefs of the Midlife Woman'. I've based the following 12 beliefs on the traditional presuppositions or 'convenient assumptions' of NLP. They form the foundation of NLP and are fundamental in assisting thousands of people to shift their own thinking patterns and thereby improve their chance of success and happiness. They are also very useful for us to apply with our children, as well as anyone we might manage or coach at work, as they are designed to empower and to give us a greater understanding of and empathy with human behaviour in general.

The Beliefs of the Midlife Woman

BELIEF 1 Everyone has a different model of the world.
WHAT IT MEANS We are all unique.
SO WHAT? It helps us understand and accept difference in others.

BELIEF 2 The meaning of your communication is the response you get.
WHAT IT MEANS Our communications are only successful if they get us the result that we want.
SO WHAT? It makes us review the approach we take to communication and encourages us to become more flexible in our style. So, if one approach doesn't work we do something different until we get the outcome we want.

BELIEF 3 There is no failure, only feedback.
WHAT IT MEANS We learn from all our experiences.

SO WHAT? If we interpret mistakes as failures, we feel defeated. If we interpret mistakes as learning opportunities, we continue to develop and have more choice. We welcome feedback.

BELIEF 4 People do the best they can with the resources they have at the time.
WHAT IT MEANS You do the best you can with what you know at that time.
SO WHAT? When we act we make the best choice we can with everything we know in that moment. Once we realise this it allows us to let go of regret and forgive others.

BELIEF 5 The person with the most flexibility will achieve the most.
WHAT IT MEANS If you don't get your result first time round, you keep doing something different until you do.
SO WHAT? By regularly practising the 8 Attitudes in this book, you will develop your thinking and your flexibility.

BELIEF 6 All behaviour has a positive intention behind it.
WHAT IT MEANS Why do people do what they do? Perhaps the mugger committed their crime to get enough money to feed their family that day. All behaviour starts with a positive intention by the person doing it. This does not necessarily mean it will also benefit the person or people that the behaviour is 'done to'.
SO WHAT? We may not agree with the behaviour, but if we look for the positive intention behind it, this allows us to have more choice in how we respond.

● CASE HISTORY: **TRICIA**

Learning to take a deep breath

This week, I heard a great example of 'Belief 6: All behaviour has a positive intention behind it' from one of my NLP practitioner students. This belief can be a challenging one to understand, but this story will help you to see exactly what it means. My student recently had her very elderly parents move in with her. She lives in a brand-new house and had spent the spring and summer building a new garden with lots of beautiful and expensive plants. In late October, while she was at work, her 91-year-old father dug up all the plants 'to get the garden ready for winter' and put them all in the recycling pile. When my client arrived home from work she discovered her lovely garden totally decimated. Her first reaction was to go mad at her old dad. Then she remembered this belief and realised that her father had dug up all her plants through positive intentions. He thought he was doing her a good turn and saving her time! That helped her to deal with the situation in a different way. She remained calm and explained that next time it wouldn't be necessary to dig them all up!

BELIEF 7 We control our minds and therefore our results.
WHAT IT MEANS We have choices about what we think and we know our thoughts influence our results.
SO WHAT? Because results are dependent on our mental state, we want to be in the best state to achieve the outcomes we want. We can change our state by changing our thoughts.

BELIEF 8 We have all the resources we need to succeed.
WHAT IT MEANS People have the capacity to be, do and have whatever they want.
SO WHAT? Most of us have largely untapped reserves of qualities, skills and attitudes that we have not yet learned to use.

BELIEF 9 The mind and body are interconnected.
WHAT IT MEANS There is a link between our thoughts and what we manifest in our bodies.
SO WHAT? We can influence our health by the way we think. That gives us hope as we can change our thoughts and see a result in our bodies.

BELIEF 10 There is a solution to every problem.
WHAT IT MEANS Finding new solutions to old problems is at the heart of creativity.
So what? This gives us confidence that we will find a way to achieve what we want.

BELIEF 11 If something isn't working, do something different.
WHAT IT MEANS If you always do what you've always done, you always get what you've always got!
SO WHAT? If your strategy isn't working, ask yourself what you can do differently next time. Keep changing your approach until you find something that works.

BELIEF 12 Anything less than 100 per cent is sabotage.
WHAT IT MEANS If you go for something in a half-hearted way you are stopping yourself from succeeding. Better to do nothing!

● EXERCISE 12
Act as if ...

For the next four weeks, take each of these 12 very powerful beliefs and act as if they are true for you. Notice how they begin to reframe your own thoughts and beliefs. For example, next time something doesn't go to plan, ask yourself: 'What can I learn from this?' As we already know, lessons should always be positive, specific to you, and to be taken on board for the future. Summarise your learnings below.

My lessons are:

....

....

....

....

....

....

....

....

....

SO WHAT? Jedi master Yoda in *Star Wars* said: 'Do, or do not. There is no try.' I tell my students this just before they embark on making changes in their lives. If they 'try' to change without committing their hearts and souls in the process, they are likely to sabotage themselves.

Just suppose for a moment that you held these 12 beliefs to be true for you. What difference would it make in your life and to your potential results? Let's explore them in more detail. I'd like to suggest that you 'try' them on for size in the context of your life and the lives of those around you. By trying them out and discovering the ones that work for you, you can, over time, turn them into beliefs and thoughts that you possess.

Remembering how to soar

There was once an eagle that got lost at birth and ended up being raised on a farm among a group of chickens. As the eagle grew up among the chickens she lived as they did and learned to accept and make the most of her chicken life. She competed with the other birds for the scraps of food that were thrown among them by the farmer. Then, one day, as she was pecking around for food with the other birds, she saw a strange yet familiar figure soaring magnificently above all the chickens.

As she watched the wonderful bird soar and glide above her, the elegant bird in the sky called down to her and said: 'I am your sister and you are an eagle just like me. You were lost and now you are found. You too are free to fly and roam the skies at will, just like me. You are destined to achieve greater things than these chickens. Come and join me now.' Being of chicken mind, the other birds urged her not to listen. 'She is not like us,' they shouted. 'Think of your responsibilities. There are nests to make and food to be collected; you have no time for flying or freedom – or for doing your own thing.' And, so the eagle continued to live her life as a chicken, believing in what chickens do. But she learned that it's not good to look too long at the sky lest another eagle appear and unsettle her by reminding her of who she really is.

Just like the eagle in this story, most of us shy away from discovering our true potential. We spend our entire lives in that place I call the 'Grey Zone'. We commit to making the most of our little lives and to being the best chickens we can be. Some people even worship those heroes that fly above them as 'gurus' or 'heroes', hoping that some day they will come to rescue them. The waste is that we do not recognise that we are just the same as the 'gurus' and that the way to freedom is simply to remember how to fly again. We were created to soar, yet we peck around like chickens. I want to share with you the easiest way to begin to fly again, and move out of the Grey Zone towards the Brilliant Zone where everything flows – and it's quite literally *impossible* to fail at anything on which we set our hearts.

Taking responsibility for your results

Are you prepared to find out what you need to do to fly like an eagle? This will involve you moving outside of the Grey Zone, even leaving your chicken friends and family behind if necessary, and taking responsibility for what you want to be, do and have for yourself.

One of the most important concepts of NLP involves 'cause and effect'. This simply means that every 'effect' on the planet starts with a 'cause'. And, every circumstance in your life is an effect. So, what's the cause? While studying women who are able to create their life the way that they want it, I noticed that they believe they are the cause of every circumstance or effect in their life. In other words, they take responsibility for whatever happens in their lives. One of our finest skills as humans is to absolve ourselves of responsibility. When something goes well, we like to take credit for it; when something goes badly, we tend to shift blame. Once we put ourselves at 'cause', and take responsibility for everything that happens to us, things will stop simply 'happening' to us, and we will actively start creating the lives that we want and deserve.

Stop for a moment to consider how you live your life. Do you generally look on the positive side of life or do you experience your life as being hard work and difficult? More crucially, perhaps, are you someone who takes responsibility for whatever happens to you in your life, or are you someone who blames others or circumstances when things go wrong?

Being at 'effect'

Living life at 'effect' literally means that you live your life at the 'effect' of everything around you. You sit around waiting for things to happen without taking responsibility for making anything happen yourself. You blame others when things do not go your way. You make excuses and find reasons why you cannot do what you want to do. It is a disempowering way to live your life because as long as you put the blame outside of yourself there is no possibility of finding a solution. If you wait and hope for things to improve or for others to provide for your wellbeing, you are a victim of your circumstances. It's no fun for others to always be around someone who is constantly moaning about their problems. Those women at 'effect' give away their power because they always look outside of themselves for the solution. They see themselves or live their lives as victims because they believe they have no choices. However, the reality is that they have chosen not to take any responsibility for their actions. Women in the Grey Zone tend to be at effect because they do not believe that it's possible to live their lives any other way. They often create so many excuses for themselves that they still walk away proudly slapping themselves on the back – even when they do not get the result they wanted. For example, a disillusioned wife at 'effect' in a loveless marriage may dream of leaving, yet she is likely to find all the excuses under the sun why it's not possible – no money, the children, loss of friends, and so on. In some ways it could be argued that it's easier to lead your whole life on the 'effect' side. You do not get the results you want, but the good thing is that there is always somebody else to blame!

● CASE HISTORY: **LUCY**

Taking control of your own body

Lucy was overweight and had dieted many times over the years. In fact, the last time she lost over four stone (about 56lbs, or 25kg) on the latest fad diet to come out of California. It was fantastic being slim, yet after a while she began to revert to her old habits. In the end it was tragic, as she regained all the weight she'd lost – and more. She came to me, distraught and desperate to lose the weight again. In fact, I was her last stop before having a gastric band fitted. I was so glad that she sought

➤

my help. Having a gastric band fitted is an example of the ultimate 'effect' behaviour. I told Lucy that having a major operation to shrink the size of your stomach so you cannot eat is like admitting that you have absolutely no control over yourself; you are like a baby again with no control over bodily functions. This may sound harsh, but I wanted to shock her into taking responsibility for her own life.

I worked with her to create a vision of what she wanted, and we planned a new healthy eating and exercise regime – one that was gradual and achievable. We also worked on solving the underlying psychological reasons why she had unconsciously sabotaged herself in the past. This made all the difference, as Lucy discovered that on an unconscious level her weight covered up for her very low confidence and self-esteem. We worked together to change her belief patterns about herself. Lucy lost her four stone again and this time she has kept it off. She has permanently changed the way she leads her life as far as food and exercise goes. She loves what she has achieved and she relishes being back in control of her life.

I am shocked by the number of people in the UK who are unable to take responsibility for their weight. You might challenge me on that and say that it's far too simplistic a viewpoint. Yet is it? The number of people having NHS stomach surgery leapt by 41 per cent between 2006 and 2007, and official records show that there were 3,459 such operations last year, up from 2,448 the year before. What's more, this total does not include the soaring number of private procedures performed in Britain and abroad. The British Obesity Surgery Society, for example, claims that there is a backlog of about 60,000 patients needing a gastric bypass – and that more NHS surgical training and resources are needed to catch up.

While completing the research for this book, I interviewed an orthopaedic surgeon, who told me about some of his obese clients who come in for surgical procedures such as new hip and knee joints, and gastric bands. He explained how many of them are in complete denial about over-eating – they make excuses about why they are overweight and dispute that it's anything to do with their own actions. Over the last 10 years, the average age of his clients needing joint replacements has reduced considerably. It is no longer unusual for someone in their 40s to have a hip replacement. They blame it on things like: 'It's genetic', 'none of the diets work for me' or 'exercise makes me ill'!

If that's not bad enough, leading health charity Diabetes UK warned that the number of people diagnosed with diabetes in the UK has risen by more than 167,000 since 2008, bringing the total diabetes population to almost 2.5 million – according to new data from GP practices. This rise is more than double the 2006 to 2007 increase of 83,000. Around 90 per cent of people with diabetes have Type 2 diabetes, which is strongly linked to lifestyle factors such as being overweight or obese, leading a sedentary lifestyle and eating an unhealthy diet. There is no getting away from the fact that this large increase is linked to the obesity crisis. There seem to be an awful lot of people who are unwilling to take responsibility for their own wellbeing.

Living life at 'cause'

In contrast, women who live their life at 'cause' take personal responsibility for everything that happens to them. Now I don't know if we *do* create everything in our lives, but accepting that we do puts us in a position of power over everything around us. More than anything else, this singular action helps us to step up our game. That's because whatever occurs in our lives, good or bad, we are focused on what there is to learn from that situation. We will feel much more in control of our lives because we are taking responsibility. The result is that we keep our own personal power in any situation.

Anyone moving from 'effect' to 'cause' feels empowered and stronger than they did before. Much of NLP is effectively designed to put us back at 'cause'. Those of us on the 'cause' side are always searching inside for a solution and to learn from our mistakes. This can sometimes seem like a tougher journey than the one experienced by those people at 'effect' in the Grey Zone – and, yet, it is one over which we keep complete control. Those at 'effect' keep their heads in the sand by blaming others for their own shortcomings. I prefer to keep control of my own destiny no matter how tough the lessons can be at times. Women at 'cause' are decisive in creating what they want in their lives. They understand that this life is not a rehearsal. If things are not happening as they would like, they learn from their experiences and move on to new possibilities. Above all, they believe they have choices in what they do and how they react to people and events.

If you want to move from the 'effect' to the 'cause' side of the equation, the first step is to remove all of your excuses. This can be a less-than-comfortable process at first; however, I guarantee that once you begin to get your results you will feel differently. From now on, you must ask yourself the following questions when things in your life do not go quite to plan:

- How have I managed to create this situation in my life and for what purpose?
- What is there for me to learn from this?
- What do I need to do differently next time?

Soon you will notice that asking yourself these questions will begin to get you different results. When you ask these questions you may notice answers popping into your mind. That's great, because they are bubbling up from your unconscious mind and you should pay attention to whatever you hear.

The mind–body connection

People at 'cause' often ask me if I believe that we also create illness in our lives. I tell them that I believe we do not create illness consciously – that makes no sense. However, our unconscious mind creates things to which we need to pay attention, and I do believe that emotional issues can have a very adverse effect on the body. It is not uncommon for physical illness to improve or even disappear once a particular emotional issue has been resolved. When I work with people who are ill, I ask them the reason why they have created an illness in their lives. The answers they provide are amazing.

There is a connection between the mind and the body, so why should it not be possible that illness has a psychological initiation? Candice Pert, who holds a research professorship in the Department of Physiology and Biophysics at Georgetown University School of Medicine in Washington, recently appeared in the film *What the Bleep* and wrote, in the book *Molecules of Emotion*: 'For many of us, and certainly for most of the medical establishment, bringing the mind too close to the body threatens the legitimacy of any particular illness, suggesting it may be imaginary, unreal, unscientific ... I've come to believe that virtually all illness, if not psychosomatic in foundation, has a definite psychosomatic component.'

Furthermore, in the book *Ageless Body, Timeless Mind*, Deepak Chopra wrote: 'Our cells are constantly eavesdropping on our thoughts and being changed by them.'

Very simply, our thoughts release chemicals into the bloodstream that literally change the construct of our cells. No wonder, then, that relentless, negative thoughts can lead to disease in the body. In fact, there is evidence to suggest that recent widows are twice as likely to develop breast cancer and that the chronically depressed are four times more likely to get sick. In both cases, negative mental states are converted into the biochemicals that create disease.

Learning from experience and healing our lives

Of course, the really interesting point is that is that if we, on some unconscious level, create something that looks like a disease, we also have the potential to *un-create* it. We are able to do this once we have learned everything there is to learn from our situation. As a reminder, what you learn should always be:

● Specific to you
● For the future

● Positive (remember our nervous system cannot process negatives)

For example, let's take a scenario where you are ill and you believe that your illness stems from the fact that you are miserable in your relationship but your husband threatens to do some harm to himself if you leave him. If you decide that your husband shouldn't emotionally blackmail you any more, this decision fails on two counts – it is for someone else and it is framed in the negative. However, coming to the conclusion that you will take responsibility for making some specific changes in your relationship as a first step fits all criteria. These are very important distinctions.

● CASE HISTORY: **CAROL**

Living on the 'cause' side of life

One of my NLP Master Practitioners, Carol, broke her wrist after falling heavily while being spun around wildly during a dance class. She was taken to the hospital and was told that she had broken the scafoid bone in her wrist, which can take anything up to 18 weeks to heal. Her wrist was X-rayed at the hospital, the break was confirmed, and her wrist was set in plaster. At that point, Carol had only just started her own corporate training and coaching business. As she was unable to drive to her clients' offices, she spent the next 10 days before her hospital appointment at home. She decided to use all of her NLP skills to focus on healing her wrist. Every

➤

day she went through intense meditation and guided visualisation, sending healing energy to her swollen wrist. She imagined her wrist healthy again. She also put herself at 'cause' and asked herself what there was to learn from the accident.

Each day she went through the same routine. At the time, she told me that she could feel her wrist getting warm as she went through the visualisation and learning process. She also surrounded herself with positive people who believed that what she was doing was possible. For a time, Carol also decided to distance herself from those people close to her who thought she should let nature take its course. Ten days later she was taken back to the hospital for the doctor to check how her wrist was healing. The plaster was removed as part of the assessment and her wrist was X-rayed again. Imagine the look on the doctor's face when there was no sign of the break on the second X-ray. All they could find was a small amount of scar tissue. When Carol asked about the original X-ray, on which the break had showed up clearly, she was told that it must have been wrong or had got mixed up with another patient's! Of course Carol knew the true story. Within two weeks of the original accident, Carol was back at work and driving again. She has never had any trouble with her wrist since.

Carol's story is an amazing example of what you can achieve if you believe that it is possible. Visualisation alone is not enough because it is important to learn from the experience as well. Carol realised that her accident was an unconscious attempt to sabotage her new business because she didn't quite believe that she could make a good living by herself. The understanding Carol developed about her own power and potential to heal her body meant that she now believed she could achieve whatever she wanted in her business, too. Her broken wrist was a wonderful metaphor for stepping into her power and moving forwards with confidence.

● EXERCISE 13
Four steps to life at 'cause'

You now have an opportunity to live your life at 'cause' for one month. If you're not sure what to do at first, just pretend – act 'as if'. Enjoy the experience and reflect on what you're learning.

- **Step 1.** Be at 'cause' in your universe. This means no more excuses! Take responsibility for everything that happens in your life.
- **Step 2.** Whatever happens to you, good or bad, ask yourself for what purpose did you create that situation in your life and what there is for you to learn from that situation. Go with what comes to you.
- **Step 3.** Reflect on what you have learned from

➤

these situations. Do something different if you need to.

- **Step 4.** Keep focusing on what you want to create in your life. Go for it!

Remember who is responsible for your success ... it's YOU! When you take 100 per cent responsibility for your life, amazing things begin to happen.

ATTITUDE 3

I Know
Who I Am

This Attitude is all about finding out what you are passionate about, because doing so goes a long way towards helping you discover your sense of self – and thereby increasing your confidence and self-esteem. When we allow ourselves to discover what we are passionate about, we experience the triumph of love and hope over fear. Remember the last time you felt real passion? That was the *real* you. If it was more than a month ago, you've got some work to do!

After years of prioritising husbands, families and careers, many women begin to feel that they don't know who they are any more. It's almost as if we have given so much of ourselves to others over the years that our true self has become diluted and, for some, unrecognisable. This can lead to a lack of confidence, assertiveness and independence that prevents us from moving forwards. This Attitude is all about regaining a sense of self, a feeling of knowing who you are at your core. You will be given all the tools you need to work this out. So, if you're ready to make some interesting discoveries, read on.

One of my mentors, Peggy Dylan, wrote the following poem about women stepping into their power on the journey of life. She wrote it at the time of the winter solstice, to express the inevitable light that follows the dark. I'm including it as it's a great metaphor for all you midlife women who are about to take up your rightful role in the world, and take responsibility for your own lives. It also represents coming through menopause and discovering who we are at our core, as well as the power that knowledge provides to us. And by power I don't mean a testosterone macho base. I mean a spiritual strength that we develop for ourselves and share with our families and those around us. This is an inspirational and healing strength that brings us fulfilment in our lives. It's time to finally be who we want to be and to live life to the fullest, whatever that means to each of us.

Femme Vital (or Essence of Woman)

Light in darkness

Warmth in cold

In Life's tender cycle

The next part to unfold

Knowing our roots

Feeling our source

Allowing the power

Of that great force

Feeling the strength

Of healing desire

Women alive

Dancing on fire

How do I spend my time?

The first step in discovering who you are is to work out how you spend your time right now. That will give you your current priorities. These may surprise or even shock you. You can then decide whether you are spending your time doing what you want to do and becoming who you want to become.

● **EXERCISE 14**
Where's my focus?

For the next week I recommend that you keep a diary of your key activities. For example, record how much time you spend on each of the following: quality time with your family (e.g., eating a meal together or going out on a family trip); quality time with your partner (e.g., going out for dinner); leisure activities (e.g., watching TV, reading, etc.); work; housework; friends; fitness; and focused time for yourself (e.g., going clothes shopping, health & fitness activities). Each day, fill in the table below, writing down a brief summary of what you did and how long you spent doing it. At the end of the week, add up the total time for each activity and note where your focus currently lies. If you like, you can work out the percentages for each activity, assuming a total of 119 waking hours during the week or 17 waking hours per day.

➤

A 2008 survey undertaken by the US Bureau of Labor looked into the way people use their time, and it uncovered some interesting results. For example, in an average day 83 per cent of women and 66 per cent of men spent some time doing household activities, while watching TV accounted for 50 per cent of leisure time for both men and women. Adults with children between the ages of 6 and 17 spent on average 46 minutes a day providing primary childcare to those children. (Primary childcare is care given as a main activity and includes physical care of, reading to or talking with children.)

I wonder what surprises you might discover about yourself! Be honest when you complete the table; don't write what you think you *should* be spending your time doing.

DAY	1	2	3	4	5	6	7	TOTAL
Quality time with family								
Quality time with partner								
Leisure activities								
Work								
Housework								

DAY	1	2	3	4	5	6	7	TOTAL
Friends								
Fitness								
Me time								

The first question to ask yourself is whether you are happy with your results. What do they say about you at the moment? Do they begin to define who you are in a way that you'd like to be defined? Is your focus where it ought to be? And, if it isn't, which areas would you like to devote more or less of your time to? Set yourself some goals and begin to rebalance your time.

● CASE HISTORY: **DIANA**

Tough love: Part I

Diana was 48 when she came to see me, and she was exhausted. She had just remarried and lived with her grown-up children (aged 23 and 20) and her husband's children (aged 17 and 20). There was no sign of any of the children leaving home. She loved nothing more than spending time with her new family, and having people around who needed her. Despite working full-time, she spent much of her time at home caring for the five adults who lived with her. She washed and ironed all their clothes and cooked a meal from scratch every night of the week. She was very house-proud and spent the weekends cleaning the house from top to bottom and changing all the beds.

One day, one of her closest friends came over for dinner. Her friend was shocked to hear the eldest of all the kids asking his mother how to turn on the washing machine! She asked Diana how much 'me time' she took for herself each week. Diana thought about it for a while and realised that she had none. In contrast, her family and new husband enjoyed the fruits of her labour and had time on their hands to have fun. In fact, Diana had got herself into a real double bind as her new husband was also moaning that she never went out with him and was becoming boring!

It's no wonder she was tired when she came to see me. I got her to do the exercise above, and she was really shocked by her results. Across the week, they looked something like this:

Family: 4 hours
Partner: 7 hours
Leisure activities/TV: 15 hours (mainly TV)
Work: 36 hours
Housework: 28 hours
Friends: 3 hours
Fitness: 0 hours
Me time: 0 hours

The first thing to do was to reduce the hours she spent working at home. She held a family meeting and announced that as there were 6 adults in the house, they would each be given tasks to do on behalf of the whole family. A family rota was established, with each person doing his or her share of all the household chores. Despite some early moans and groans, the other family members soon got used to the new rotas and Diana realised that she had been holding the kids back by doing everything for them. She began going out with her husband on a 'date night' at least once a week – and having more fun. The amount of quality time for her partner and herself was going up and her housework going down! It was a good start.

Which goddess are you?

The next step in your quest to be authentic is to complete a quiz that will help you to discover who you are at your core. It will reveal the main energies at play within us, and how they drive and impact upon our behaviour. However, this is no *Cosmo* quiz. It is a psychological questionnaire to help you better understand yourself by identifying the different and sometimes contradictory themes that shape your life.

The concept of archetypes was originally created by the psychologist Carl Jung in the early 20th century. He had based his ideas on the work of Plato. An archetype is a model of a personality type and their behaviours, and archetypes are held unconsciously in our psyche. Jung's archetypes are universal – they can be found across many different cultures and are used to observe and analyse behaviour. Completing the questionnaire on page 94 raises our archetypes to a level of conscious awareness where we can decide if we are happy with them. If not, they can be worked on and changed.

I have taken 6 well-known goddesses from folklore and utilised them as 'archetypical females'; each represents a particular way of interpreting events and acting in the world. For example, Athena is the competitive, results-orientated warrior goddess whereas Demeter is the selfless carer, putting others before herself. The risk is that if you are not consciously aware of how these archetypes act out in your life, they may end up running you. Left unacknowledged, they can also create internal conflict. People often live out an unsatisfactory archetypal script because they have no idea how to change it.

The use of the 'Goddess Archetype Indicator', or GAI ©, will enable you to change more rapidly. The simple act of completing the questionnaire and knowing which archetypes are strongest in your life will give you more choices about who you want to be in future. I've been testing this questionnaire with groups of my female audiences over the last year and the results have been spookily accurate. Do bear in mind, however, that your results should be taken as an indicator of type rather than a firm fact. You may also notice that some of your archetypes are your 'core', whereas others will flow in and out of your life depending upon what is going on for you at that moment.

For example, my own strongest archetype is Athena, the warrior. I recognise this energy in myself, as well as the accompanying behaviours I demonstrate, as I have spent all my life competing in a male-dominated environment, battling to be recognised. At the moment, my father is sick and I am spending more of my time caring for him and my mother. I have called in my Demeter archetype to help me to cope with this family crisis. Being consciously aware of this now, I have choices about whether I want to keep more of this Demeter energy in my life in the longer term. We can all learn to call on different archetypes to assist us with particular life tasks, if we know how to do that. I will show you how.

● EXERCISE 15
The GAI ©

Work as quickly as possible, as your first reaction is often your best response. Answer all of the questions. If you are unsure of an answer, do your best, based on your understanding of the question and then move on. Answer what is generally true f or you. Answer the questions truthfully – as you are right now rather than how you'd like to be in future or as someone else would like you to be. Remember that all six goddess archetypes are equally valuable in our lives and each brings with it unique gifts. No one archetype is better or worse than another. Therefore, there are no right or wrong answers.

There are 36 questions. Give each question a score from 1 to 5 in the shaded box and then total each column at the bottom of the page. You will be left with six total scores, each of which adds up to a maximum of 30 points. Note your highest and lowest total scores and the initials at the top of the columns. Then turn to the definitions and discover your highest and lowest goddess archetypes.

➤

Goddess Archetype Indicator

Please score each question as follows in the shaded box:

1 = strongly disagree, 2 = disagree, 3 = neutral,
4 = agree, 5 = strongly agree

	At	Dem	Ap	Ar	Hera	Psy
1. I'm prepared to work long hours in order to achieve my result						
2. I prefer being at home with the family than going out						
3. I love dressing up to go out and enjoy wearing sexy clothes						
4. I prefer living in the country closer to nature than in the centre of town						
5. I prefer to be in control of situations around me						
6. I like to transform situations and people						
7. I am more connected to my thoughts and ideas than to my feelings						
8. I find fulfilment through assisting others						
9. I am more complete when I am in love						

	At	Dem	Ap	Ar	Hera	Psy
10. I never feel settled				�		
11. I take my responsibilities seriously					▓	
12. I go by my intuitions regularly						▓
13. I enjoy intellectual conversation	▓					
14. I find it difficult to say no		▓				
15. Having a great body is really important to me			▓			
16. Regular exercise and physical fitness is a high priority in my life				▓		
17. I take over when others flounder around me					▓	
18. I enjoy changing things around me						▓
19. I take personal risks to get what I want	▓					
20. I often put the needs of others above my own		▓				

	At	Dem	Ap	Ar	Hera	Psy
21. I can't resist looking at my reflection when I pass a mirror			■			
22. I love to walk in nature				■		
23. I'm good at getting others to do things					■	
24. I find it easy to come up with creative ideas						■
25. I am very goals and results focused	■					
26. I love to cook and prepare fresh food	■					
27. I adore romantic surprises			■			
28. I'm very fond of many types of animals				■		
29. I've been told that I have leadership qualities					■	
30. I spend time discovering my spiritual side						■
31. I get what I want in life most of the time	■					

	At	Dem	Ap	Ar	Hera	Psy
32. I've always put my family before my career		■				
33. I'd consider surgery to keep my looks as long as possible			■			
34. I enjoy working in my garden				■		
35. I'm always being asked by friends and colleagues to organise things					■	
36. I take time for myself regularly						■
TOTALS:						

Interpreting your results

You now have a total value assigned to each archetype. Transfer your scores to the blank wheel on page 99. For each archetype, shade in the appropriate area in the wheel that corresponds to the number value. For example, if the value next to Athena is 22, shade in the Athena section of the wheel from 22 to the centre of the wheel. Do this for all 6 archetypes.

You should first note the archetype that you scored highest. This is the archetype that is most influential in

➤

Example GAI © Wheel

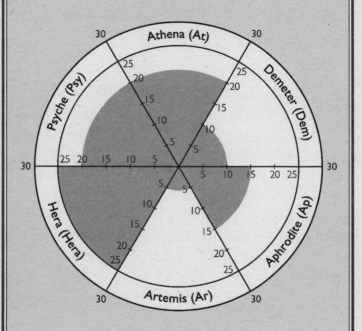

your life right now. Your scores will change over time and are likely to be influenced by significant events in your life at the time you complete the questionnaire. However, though your score may fluctuate, your strongest archetype is likely to remain unchanged.

A score of 24–30 is very high, 18–23 is moderately high, 12–17 is mid-range to low, and anything below 12 is very low. Then notice your second highest score, as this archetype is also likely to be active in your life. If you had

Your GAI © Wheel

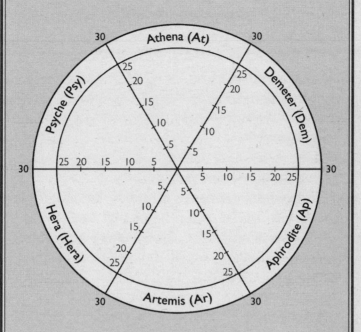

two highest scores that are the same, then it is very likely that both these archetypes are very active in your life right now. Next, notice your lowest score. This is the archetype that is least active in your life and the one on which you may wish to focus – calling in more of that energy. Consider if it would be useful for you to have more of that energy in your life, and review the following descriptions of each archetype to see the individual energies that characterise each, and how specifically you can achieve them.

To make it easier, I've prepared an example wheel for you to see how it's done (see previous page). This woman has a very high score for Hera, and moderately high scores for Athena and Psyche. This suggests that she is a very focused person, with strong organisational and leadership capabilities. She is good at getting the best out of people. However, she might well need to spend more time having fun and relaxing, and enjoying time with those close to her.

The 6 goddess archetypes

Here is a brief description of each archetype, where you'll find: details of their strengths and problem areas; ways of calling that archetype into your life; and, examples of women who display or have displayed that archetype.

ATHENA (AT)
● **Description:** This is the ambitious career woman. Athena faces problems head on and defends the boundaries of her family and community to which she belongs. She sets and sticks to goals and develops plans to reach those goals by force or persuasion. She has high levels of discipline and enjoys competing. She is great to have on your side.
● **Theme:** Nothing is impossible.
● **Strengths:** Self-reliant, goal-orientated, tenacious, industrious, intellectual, competitive, stands up for what she believes is right.

● **Issues:** Has a tendency to be selfish, ruthless, arrogant, controlling.

● **How to increase this archetype in you:** Set some goals and stick to them, step up your own personal development, take more 'me time', read some serious non-fiction books, go to the gym regularly, speak your mind, make decisions (even small ones!), put yourself first for a change.

● **Examples:** Anita Roddick (founder of The Body Shop), Dame Ellen MacArthur (yachtswoman), Marjorie Scardino (first female Chief Executive of a FTSE 100 company, when she was appointed CEO of Pearson in 1997).

DEMETER (DEM)

● **Description:** This is the nurturing caregiver or parent who, through empathy and commitment, is able to create a safe and nurturing environment. She encourages community spirit and nurturing relationships among others.

● **Theme:** I'll go to the ends of the earth for you.

● **Strengths:** Deeply caring, mother-earth type, well-organised, selfless, strong resolve. Provides emotional nurturing, guidance and teaching, and performs maintenance tasks such as housework, etc.

● **Issues:** Lives her life through others, loss of self to the point of martyrdom. Can also smother those around her and prevent them from developing fully. Her failure to set boundaries can result in exhaustion.

- **How to increase this archetype in you:** Slow down, give your family and friends your time, cook a meal from scratch, do some voluntary work, invite your friends over for dinner.
- **Examples:** Mother Teresa, Princess Diana, Nigella Lawson.

APHRODITE (AP)

- **Description:** The beautiful, outgoing lover who enjoys connectedness, bonding and passionate commitment. Aphrodite loves life and enjoys life as an intense and seductive experience. She loves to be in love.
- **Theme:** I'm worth it.
- **Strengths:** Self-love, fun-loving, playful, generous, sexual, considers the body to be sacred, romantic, passionate, loves and sponsors the arts.
- **Issues:** Has a tendency to be inauthentic, self-centred, doesn't care about the consequences of her passions, experiences a love of self that can develop into addiction.
- **How to increase this archetype in you:** Take the time to have a facial and massage, drink champagne while having a luxurious bubble bath, buy new lingerie, turn your bedroom into a boudoir, start some new hobbies where you will meet new men (e.g., salsa dancing, golf).
- **Examples:** Jordan (glamour model and TV personality), Marilyn Monroe, Sophia Loren.

ARTEMIS (AR)

- **Description:** Seeks the answer. She possesses an introverted and independent temperament, represents the goddess of nature and is concerned with matters of the outdoors, animals, environmental protection and women's communities. She is practical, adventurous, athletic and prefers solitude. She symbolises regenerative earth power over all living things.
- **Theme:** I'll do it my way.
- **Strengths:** Spirituality, adventuress, huntress, lover of wilderness, enjoys spending time in nature and with animals, prepared to make changes to her life if things are not working.
- **Issues:** Detached from reality, loner, too independent, likes change for the sake of change.
- **How to increase this archetype in you:** Spend time in nature, sponsor an animal, go mountaineering or canoeing, buy a bike, change something important, start to meditate.
- **Examples:** Dr Dian Fossey (scientist who spent her life studying gorillas in Africa), Dr Charlotte Uhlenbroek (TV traveller and zoologist), Jane Goodall (famous chimpanzee expert).

HERA (HERA)

- **Description:** Takes charge of the kingdom around her. She possesses an ability to rule with vision and to empower others in the process. She is extroverted and takes power and control, especially when others do not. She also represents the goddess of marriage, concerned with partnership and her relationship as wife to a man. She faces life challenges regarding power, status and leadership.

- **Theme:** Let me sort it out.
- **Strengths:** Empress, ruler, wife, worldly power, tradition, marriage, partnership, morality, matriarch.
- **Issues:** Over-powering, bossy, walks over those seen as weak. Can be too quick to punish and always wants more power.
- **How to increase this archetype in you:** Volunteer to take charge of something, delegate to others, tell others about your vision, talk more to others about your views of the world generally, and spend more time on your intimate relationship.
- **Examples:** Hillary Clinton, Sharon Osborne, Indira Ghandi.

PSYCHE (PSY)
- **Description:** Teacher, healer, catalyst for change whose power is to transform her own personal reality as well as the reality of others. She is good at getting the best out of others, often through an experience of her own suffering and subsequent healing.
- **Theme:** Listen to your heart and follow your dreams.
- **Strengths:** Visions, dreams, internal transformation, healer, psychic power, peace-loving, innovative, flexible.
- **Issues:** Unrealistic, not very grounded, leaves

unfinished business, arrogant if uses power for
own egocentric ends.
● **How to increase this archetype in you:** Slow
down and smell the flowers, forgive someone, help
someone sort out a problem, listen and act on your
intuitions, take some personal development training.
● **Examples:** Sally Morgan (psychic), Oprah
Winfrey, Louise Hay (author and founder of
Hay House Publishing).

● CASE HISTORY: **DIANA**
Tough love: Part II
Once she'd worked on getting her family onboard to help
out with the household responsibilities, and begun to make
a little time for herself, Diana's next step was to complete
the GAI © questionnaire. Which archetype do you think
was her highest? We already know that she spent many
hours looking after a family of five adults, so no it was no
real surprise that her highest score – at 28 – was Demeter.
Her second-highest score was Hera, at 22. Together, these
showed how Diana spent most of her time organising
and caring for others. However, what she hadn't noticed,
until she took the GAI © questionnaire, was that she
was actually holding herself and her grown-up kids back.
Her caring came near to smothering her family. She was
holding her children back because they were not learning

➤

to become independent adults. She was holding herself back from having the time to enjoy life to the full with her new husband. Diana's lowest score (12) was Aphrodite, and she was pretty shocked to discover how low it really was. She was very keen to call in more of that energy, or she felt that her new marriage might be at risk.

She continued to redistribute the household chores between her husband and grown-up children, splitting her 'spare' time between quality time with her husband and time for herself. She used her new time to shop for new clothes, book spa treatments and generally spoil herself. She began to feel fantastic and her husband was delighted with the result! When she retook the questionnaire 6 months later, her Aphrodite score had moved into second place behind Hera. Her Demeter archetype had moved into third place.

Consider if you are happy with your current scores and how the archetypes play out in your life. Use the exercise below to set yourself some goals.

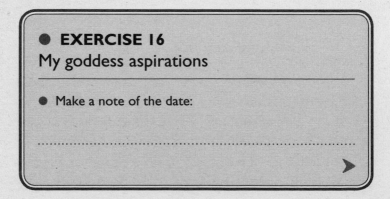

● **EXERCISE 16**
My goddess aspirations

● Make a note of the date:

Note below your goddess goals and how you are going to reduce the hold of current archetypes or increase the energy of new ones.

● The archetype I want to reduce is:

....

● I will do this by:

....

● The archetype I want to increase is:

....

● I will do this by:

....

6 to 12 months from now, retake the questionnaire to discover how far your archetypes have remained constant or how well you have done at calling new archetypes into your life.

My personal mission in life

We've worked on how you spend your time and we've identified your core goddess archetype/s. You have already begun to shift the balance of your time and your energy closer to who you really are and what you really want and deserve in your life. The last stage of the process is to work further on your purpose in life, and what will make you totally authentic or at ease with yourself. In other words, who are you, what do you do and what do you have when you are truly being yourself? This does not have to mean making a massive change in your life. However, it does mean understanding what is really important to you, what you excel at and how you can utilise these strengths more effectively than you do right now. When I was working as a business consultant in the early 2000s, I realised that although I enjoyed my work, it didn't drive my real passion in life – which was to give people more choices about how they lead their lives and the results they achieve. I first did the exercise you are about to do in 1997. It clarified what I needed to focus on for the future, and I set about achieving that goal. You should do this in your own time and at your own pace. This is a journey of discovery and something you should enjoy.

● EXERCISE 17
Who am I when I'm being authentic?

This exercise will take around an hour to complete, so make sure you have enough time to do it justice in one sitting. Make sure you do it alone, too, to ensure that you don't end up with someone else's mission!

STEP 1: WHAT MOTIVATES ME?
Go through the following lists of words and circle each one that gives you a strong positive feeling because it is important to you. Then go back and pick the top three or

four themes that have the greatest meaning in your life.
There are no correct answers, and the meaning of each
word or phrase is up to you.

Personal achievement

Winning

Happiness

Finding the good in others

Earning money

Building something

Loving someone

Gaining approval of others

Caring for others

Being loved, being accepted

Gaining recognition

Popularity

Creating something

Competence

Getting things done

Independence

Doing good

Risking

Dominating

Being different and still
fitting in

Being unique

Being your best

Reaching your potential

Gaining security, safety

Finding excitement

Controlling

Being a leader

Having fun

Learning, gaining wisdom

Working hard

Gaining mastery

Having influence over
others

Making a worthwhile
contribution

Experiencing life to its
fullest

Fully expressing yourself

Seeking adventure

Becoming an expert

Power, authority

Making a positive difference

Prestige

Developing people or
things

Increasing effectiveness

Seeing how much you can
get away with

Waiting until the last minute

If a word or phrase comes to mind that isn't on the list, please add it.

STEP 2: MY GREATEST ACCOMPLISHMENTS

Now, in each age range below, list at least one accomplishment that gave you a great sense of joy. These are accomplishments that you personally felt good about, regardless of what others thought at the time. If you can't think of anything, pass on to the next age range. Stop when you reach your current age range.

- **0–12:**
....

- **13–17:**
....

- **18–22:**
....

- **23–30:**
....

- **31–40:**
....

- **41–50:**
....

➤

- **51–60:**

....

- **60+:**

....

STEP 3: WHAT I DO BEST

After you have completed the above, please answer the following questions:

1. Throughout your life, what activity has consistently produced the greatest sense of joy and self-fulfilment for you?
2. What else is important to you about the way you live your life?
3. What skills or abilities do you have that you most like to utilise?
4. What do you most like about yourself?

What patterns, trends or similarities do you observe in your answers so far?

STEP 4: WHO ARE YOU, REALLY?

The goal of this step is to create a set of words that causes you to connect with what your life is about.

Each of the exercises in this chapter has produced information about you. Now it's time for you to choose the words, combinations of words and phrases that appear in your answers to draw up a statement of who you are at your core. I call this your statement of authenticity and it should consist of what you do best, what you are passionate about and what is most important to you. It should tempt you out of bed in the mornings and motivate you to take action towards your goals. It should have a strong meaning and deep emotional feeling for you. The key is to come up with a definite theme that best describes the driving force in your life, which you can review regularly and experience a strong emotional charge each time you do so.

For example, my statement is:

'I am brave, creative and caring. When I work well I am a catalyst for change in others. I assist them to create more choices about how they live their lives.'

Write your statement here:

....

....

....

....

....

....

....

STEP 5: VISUALISE THE AUTHENTIC YOU

As you look at your statement, notice what thoughts it conjures up in your mind. What are you seeing yourself doing, hearing yourself saying and how are you feeling? Close your eyes if it helps to get a clearer image. Make sure that you are looking through your own eyes in the picture that you have, as opposed to seeing yourself in the picture. That makes the effect much more powerful.

Notice how you can turn up the brightness of everything around you. Pretend that your mind works like a television set and you can adjust the brightness and colour controls. What sounds are associated with your picture? Again, turn up the volume control on your TV set and hear what others are saying about you and what you are saying to yourself. Notice the feelings that your thoughts create inside of you and turn up those feelings to double or triple intensity. You can do this by just turning your attention onto where those feelings are located in your body. Notice, as well, if those feelings are moving around. If they are, make them move faster and notice how this intensifies them. How does that feel? Did you notice the feelings in your image becoming more intense?

This exercise has shown us that if we intensify the colours, brightness, sounds and feelings, we can intensify our emotional response to our visualisation. The whole point of visualising our desires is to create an emotional response that sends clear and strong messages to our unconscious mind that we are serious about the changes we wish to make.

Have fun with this and play around until you find a perfect combination for increasing your mental imagery.

What now?

One of the important foundations of NLP is learning to 'act as if'. The last exercise showed you how to behave as the authentic 'you'. Ask yourself what first steps you need to take to start on your journey of authenticity. Personally, I realised that I needed to work with individuals and groups outside the risk-averse structure of a large corporation. That began the journey that has, to date, spanned over 12 years, during which time I have become a certified NLP trainer, coach and writer. 'Acting as if' is like pretending. You just pretend to be the person you really deserve to be. Think about what that person would look like, how they would dress, how they would spend their time, and what they believe about themselves. Then start to act in the same way. As we know already, the effect on our nervous system of actually doing something or imagining doing something is practically the same, which is one reason why visualisation works so well in sports. When you begin to 'act as if' you are giving your unconscious mind an important message that this outcome is possible and true for you. Because of the laws of attraction that we discussed in Attitude 2, you will begin to attract people and situations that help you to become the person you are acting out.

For example, when I started my business I gave it a name that implied 'large and successful' – The Change Corporation – and I focused on working with large corporate clients. I asked myself: 'How would a large organisation act? From my consultancy days, working for one of the largest global consulting firms, I had learned that quality was essential. Therefore, I spent my small start-up budget ensuring that our website and brochures met the very high standards you might expect from a much larger company. This worked well and has consistently been a deciding factor in our ability to successfully win business with large global companies.

Now ask yourself the following: who am I really? Am I living an authentic life? And, if not, what must I change? How can I start to 'act as if'? What's the first step for me to take?

> **Wherever you go, there you are, so enjoy living a totally authentic life. Start now.**

ATTITUDE 4

I Am True to Myself

One of the comments I hear from my midlife female clients, which concerns me more than anything else, is that they believe it's better to be secure in their lives than happy – to stay 'stuck' rather than go for something different. That often means spending their lives with the 'wrong' person because they don't want to be alone, or they want someone to look after them financially, or both. Or maybe they have spent their lives in the wrong job because it pays the bills. What a waste! They spend their lives kidding themselves that they've made the right choices while watching their lives pass them by.

The only thing keeping us stuck in a rut is fear – fear that by making a change we may end up with something not as good as what we currently have. The trouble is, living with this fear makes us lose respect for ourselves, which can lead to low self-esteem, frustration and dependency on someone else as a result.

In this chapter I'm going to show you how to alter your mindset so that you view change as something exciting rather than frightening.

Learning to respect yourself

In my experience, facing up to change is a lot less scary than you think. As I mentioned earlier, I made four key life-changing decisions in my mid-40s. At 43, I left my career and my husband within months of each other, and then started my new company. A few years later, I began to write. It's an old cliché and it's true – when one door closes another opens, especially when you are prepared to have absolute faith and do whatever it takes. *Of course* I was scared, and my family made sacrifices for a while – sacrifices like having fewer holidays and making our clothes last a bit longer. The most drastic thing we did was to downsize the house. And, now, four years later, we are benefiting from the hard work and focus. I've often wondered if I expected too much of my kids in supporting me. But, on the night of my first book launch, my daughter surprised me by giving a short speech about how much they had learned from my experiences – independence, focus and determination. Those around me respect me for being true to myself. Most importantly, I respect myself.

● CASE HISTORY: **KAREN**

Disappointing another to be true to yourself

Karen is human resources director, and on the board of a large corporation. She manages hundreds of staff, as well as a huge budget. When she had been out of a relationship for several years, she decided to experiment with internet dating. She got chatting online to Mark, who shared similar interests and experience. He was a similar age – late 40s – was divorced with no children, and, like Karen, enjoyed intellectual and artistic pursuits. They spent several weeks exchanging emails and then phone calls. One warm summer's evening they agreed to meet outside a popular London restaurant. Karen was full of anticipation and had bought a glamorous new summer outfit for the occasion. As she approached the agreed meeting place, she spotted Mark waiting for her. Her heart sunk a little as she saw him for the first time. He was tall and slim which she liked but there was no spark between them.

However, she convinced herself that he was perfect in every other way and that passion and chemistry would follow. They began a relationship that was pretty good at first. They shared many cultural pursuits and stimulating late-night conversations. A lack of sex remained an issue, but Karen was confident that it would be OK. She was enjoying being in a relationship again, which made up for a lot. She was posted overseas for a year and they continued to see each other regularly, spending their holidays together. Mark had fallen madly in love with Karen and she noticed how she avoided telling him she loved him back. On her return to the UK, Karen moved in with Mark, confident that this step would sort out the relationship. By now, there was no passion at all in the relationship, as they had stopped having any kind of physical relationship many months before. They were like

➤

brother and sister. Neither of them addressed the issues in the relationship for fear of opening Pandora's box.

When she came to see me she wanted to 'fix' the relationship, as she was desperate for it to work. She was really terrified of being alone again. We worked together over several sessions to explore what it was that she really wanted in a relationship, and then we worked on boosting her level of self-confidence and self-esteem. She was so outwardly successful and confident, yet on the inside she was terrified of being alone. Once she was clear about what was important to her in a relationship she realised that she was letting herself down to accept anything less than that. She made the break from Mark and now enjoys an exciting new single lifestyle. She would like to meet someone eventually, but she's confident now that when she settles down it will be with someone who is perfect for her.

Karen was in denial for the whole of her relationship with Mark. She so wanted him to be the 'one' that she was prepared to sacrifice her own physical needs in that relationship. She spent three years trying to put a square peg into a round hole, knowing deep down from the moment she met him that it wasn't right. Now she is much clearer about what she wants and she is prepared to wait for the 'right' one as opposed to settling for second best. Mark, though disappointed at first, has also moved on. For Karen, it wasn't fear of financial insecurity that kept her stuck; it was her fear of being alone and not finding anyone else. Ask yourself this question: 'Am I with my partner because I want to be or because I believe I have to be?' How many women do you know in a similar situation – women who are with the wrong partner, in the wrong job, or even in a stagnant friendship, because they think they *should* be? Maybe you are one of them?

● CASE HISTORY: **NADINE**
Lie back and think of England

Another of my clients came to see me, desperate to leave her relationship but for different reasons. Nadine was in her late 40s and had been married for 23 years. She was the daughter of a wealthy businessman, and her husband was a 'wheeler-dealer', always on the verge of the next big money-spinner or bankruptcy. Sadly, significant success had eluded them and all of Nadine's large inheritance from her parents had been frittered away over the years. Over a period of time, she noticed how her husband's jokes held less appeal, how the arguments were becoming more frequent, and how she began to dread his homecomings – and especially his daily demands for sex. Her self-esteem and confidence were at an all-time low. When she came to see me she had lived like this for over three years.

We worked on what was important to her in a relationship and (not surprisingly) discovered that her husband was not a good match for her on many levels. Sadly, the money was all gone and so she started to consider how she could make a living for herself after so

➤

> many years of not working. She is very creative and soon set up a small business importing jewellery from China. Once that was in place and she could begin to support herself, she asked her husband to leave. There have been many temptations to have him back, but she has remained true to her own values, and her beliefs about what is most important. Her life is not yet a 'bed of roses'; but if you were to ask her, she would tell you that she made the right choice.

Nadine was in the same situation as many midlife women who have sacrificed many years to their husbands and families. Once her children were all away at school, and she was alone far more often with her husband, the cracks soon began to appear. Although she was terrified about the future, it was still better than imagining life with a domineering and irresponsible man whom she no longer loved. Although every day is a new adventure for her, the separation has not been as traumatic as she first envisaged and even her children are delighted about the new arrangements. They too were stressed each time they came home because of all the arguments between their parents. She is even making money for herself from her new business.

Both Nadine and Karen had the courage finally to wake up to the reality of their situations and be true to themselves after many years of self-sacrifice and anguish. They were prepared to disappoint their partners in order to do what was right for them, and they have blossomed as a result. Sometimes, it may seem easier to stick your head in the sand; however, in the long term it will not bring you what you deserve. And, of course, it's your choice. You do not have to change anything that you don't want to change. You can choose to stay in the Grey Zone if you like! What I will say, though, is that often those initial steps are easier than you think.

This Attitude – I am true to myself – will focus on relationships and careers, to help you identify what is most important to you in both of these important areas of your life. You can then assess how your current relationship and career shape up. Or, if you're not in a relationship, I guarantee that you will feel much more confident about choosing the right person. What's more, you'll take the appropriate steps to make sure that the relationship you *do* choose will be more successful in the long term. If you're at a crossroads in your career, or wanting to embark upon a new one, this Attitude will help you make the right decisions. Once you are familiar with the process, you can use the same technique for other areas of your life, too.

We are going to find out what's most important to us in both our relationship and our career by discovering our core personal values in these areas.

The power of values

Our values determine how we spend our time. They are the reason that we do what we do. They motivate us to take action and they are the means by which we evaluate ourselves after the event, and decide if we did a good job – or, indeed, the right thing. Our values also provide our moral code, so if we feel uncomfortable about anything we've done it's likely to be due to a conflict of values.

In other words, our values are what are most important to us – and, yet, they are largely unconscious. We know they are there, though, whenever we start to feel uneasy about something. For example, if I'm uncomfortable being with a partner who is very controlling, one of my values is likely to be independence. Or, if I'm miserable doing a routine 9 to 5 job, having flexibility is likely to be one of my values. The trouble is that as our values are largely unconscious, we do not know what they are. As a result, we may drift into careers and relationships that are not aligned with our values. We often discover this after the fact, when there is a clash between what is going on around us and how we feel on the inside. This manifests as an inner conflict that leads to us feel unhappy or even ill – and often we don't know why.

Just imagine, then, if you were to be able to define your values consciously and have them as a 'checklist' for yourself. You would make much better decisions and be much happier in how you spend your time and whom you spend it with. You would even have the choice to change your values, which would have a powerful impact on your life.

Where do our values come from?

Our values are instilled in us at an early age, most often before the age of 7. At this age our surroundings are imprinted upon us with little of our own filtering. For example, our values will be influenced by the values of our parents, close family, environment, school, and everything and everyone else that touches our lives. Our values determine the way we think and how we behave. If you want to find out what your values are, then ask yourself what was important to those around you when you were growing up. It's likely that you have adopted many of their values.

For example, I was brought up in the East End of London where the values of family and community were important. However, before you start to panic at the thought of having adopted your parents' values, it's also important to understand that our values change and can be changed. If you are a parent, I guarantee that on the day your first child was born your values will have changed. This happens unconsciously. Other times in our lives when our values are likely to change include marriage, divorce, bereavement, redundancy, retirement, illness and so on.

Aligning your values to your goals

I am going to show you how to become consciously aware of your values. Then we'll move on to helping you understand how they impact on your life and what you achieve. If you so wish, you can then decide to change them. And, if your values are aligned to your goals, it will become much easier to achieve them. I spent 11 years as a business consultant for one of the top four global consulting houses. It was a great job, which was well paid and involved lots of travel. But I was never totally happy in that job. I discovered that my values around spirituality, entrepreneurship, personal development, risk-taking and being my own boss were not being addressed in my consulting role. When I discovered this, I was able to assess what kind of career would meet my needs. That's when I decided to start my own business, as it ticked all the boxes in terms of what is most important to me.

If we identify and pay attention to our values, we will quickly learn how to be true to ourselves and get a clearer idea of where we want to go over the next stage of our lives. We will begin by identifying your relationship values, as your intimate relationship is likely to be one of the key areas of your life (see page 17). This will be an invaluable learning process for you, whether you are in a relationship or not. Once you have learned the process, you can then apply it to other areas of your life. For example, you can use it to find out if you are in the right career by eliciting your career values, or find out what's important to your wellbeing by eliciting your health and fitness values.

Are you ready to learn something really exciting about yourself?

Your relationship values

Your relationship values are the things that are most important to you about your intimate relationship. These should not be based on the relationship you are in now but, rather, your ideal relationship. Of course, if your relationship is good then many of these values will overlap. That is absolutely fine.

● **EXERCISE 18**
My relationship values

When eliciting your relationship values it's best to find someone who can work with you to ask you the questions. This should *not* be your intimate partner; instead, choose a friend who can act as your coach for this exercise. You should ask them to keep going with the questioning, even when your answers dry up. This is because your conscious

➤

---

values come out first, as they are at surface level. Your unconscious values and those that you are least aware of are likely to come out later and may prove to be the most important of all the values you identify.

STEP I: ELICITATION

Get your exercise partner to ask you the following question: 'What's important to you about your relationship?' Your partner must write down the words that you say and not suggest any answers, as those are their own values, not yours. In NLP, the words we are listening for are called 'nominalisations'. A nominalisation is a verb (process word) that has been transformed into an abstract noun. For example, 'communicate' becomes 'communication', or 'relate' becomes 'relationship'. Nominalisations are therefore words that refer to things you cannot see or touch. Exceptions to this rule are money and sex! Also, listen out for answers such as 'going out with friends'. That is not a nominalisation. In these cases your partner would ask: 'What does going out with friends do or get for you?' You might then say: 'It gives me some freedom in my relationship'. Freedom is the value. See the sample question-and-answer session below.

You must tell your exercise partner to expect a first and second 'wave' of values from you. The first wave is those values at a more conscious level of awareness. Once these cease to flow, your exercise partner should continue with the questioning and you must pay attention to whatever comes into your mind. These are your unconscious values.

For example, when you are asked what is important to you about your relationship, you say in quick succession:

- Love
- Sharing
- Communication
- Sex
- Security
- Learning
- Inspiration
- Independence

You then say 'going out'. This is not a value, so your partner asks you: 'What does going out do or get for you?' You say 'Fun'. This is the value. Add 'fun' to your list.

You then say you can't think of any more. That means you are at the end of the first wave. Your partner carries on regardless, to get your second wave or those values at a more unconscious level. You then say:

- Trust
- Reliability
- Honesty
- Authenticity
- Permanence

So, five more values were identified from the second wave. You then couldn't think of any more values, so step I is finished.

STEP 2: THRESHOLD VALUES

Your partner should show you all the values you have provided and ask you: 'If you had all these values met by your partner, is there anything else that would cause you to leave for someone new?'

Your partner should note down any new values that you mention and continue to question you until you come up with repeat words. Any new values should also be added to your list.

STEP 3: HIERARCHY OF VALUES

Your exercise partner should now give you the list of values and ask you to pick the top 8, and then rank them in order of priority. This may seem a challenge, and yet it is important to understand the most important through to the least important.

STEP 4: REWRITE YOUR LIST

Your exercise partner should then rewrite your list in the order you have given. You may find that some of your most important values came out in the second wave of elicitation. This is quite common and means that some of your most important values were those at an unconscious level.

If we go back to our example, love is still the number 1 value, authenticity has moved to number 2, inspiration moved to number 3, sharing went to number 4, communication is now number 5, sex is number 6, honesty is number 7, and fun shifted to number 8. Authenticity and honesty were from the second wave, and became very important values in this example.

- Love
- Authenticity
- Inspiration
- Sharing
- Communication
- Sex
- Honesty
- Fun

STEP 5: TEST

You may feel that your values are in the right order. However, your exercise partner should check them as follows. Your partner starts with value number 1 (the most important) and asks (using our example): 'Assuming you could have love (value number 1) but not authenticity (value number 2), would that be OK with you?'

They need to force a choice from you. If you say it is OK, then those values are in the right order. If you say it's not OK, the values need to be reversed – in other words, number 2 becomes number 1 and vice versa. Your partner then checks value number 2 against number 3 until you get to the end of the 8 values. You can then be sure that they are in the right order.

STEP 6: HOW DOES YOUR RELATIONSHIP STACK UP?

If you are not in a relationship and would like to be, this list will be invaluable to you in making a better choice next time. Why? Because you will be seeking the person who meets your values, or at least meets the majority of the values most important to you. If they don't meet them. there will always be challenges for you. For example, if your most important value is freedom and theirs is control, you will have a problem on your hands.

You can even ask a potential partner the elicitation question if you want to be sure that you are both on the same page. When I'm interested in a guy, I always ask him: 'What's important to you about a relationship?' and I listen carefully to what he says!

If you are in a relationship, I suggest that you go through your list of 8 values and score your current relationship out of 10 against each value. See the example below for guidance.

- Love   8/10
- Authenticity   7/10
- Inspiration   3/10
- Sharing   3/10
- Communication   2/10
- Sex   9/10
- Honesty   8/10
- Fun   9/10

I normally break the scores into three categories:

0–4	High risk area for the relationship
5–7	Medium risk area for the relationship
8–10	Low risk area for the relationship

In our example, this couple are in love, have great sex and fun, but their relationship could be much better in the areas of inspiration, sharing and communication. Because these three are all important values for this person, we could predict this relationship will run into trouble in the longer term – once the initial lust wears off – unless they can work on the weaker areas.

Ask yourself where the high and medium risk areas of your relationship are. If any of these match your top three values, then you have some work to do. It's important that you work on these with your partner. Awareness and motivation often creates enough momentum for change, and you can resolve the problematic issues by having an open and honest discussion about what needs to change. If this is not possible, you may need to seek assistance from an NLP coach like myself, or from an organisation like Relate.

One of my NLP teachers, Tad James, told me once to ask this important question first: *'Is this relationship worth saving?'*

This question saves a lot of time. If you believe it is, then go for it and do whatever it takes to save it. If it isn't, then ask yourself what the emotional cost of staying might be. What would the answer be if you were being totally true to yourself?

Other tips about values

Notice if any of the relationship values that you elicited were phrased as a negative. For example, 'I don't want to be alone'. In NLP, this is an example of what is called an 'away-from' value. That's because you are moving away from what you don't want as opposed to moving towards what you want. In contrast, 'I want to have fun' is a 'towards' value. Both of these examples will create motivation for you. However, the motivation is fundamentally different. 'Away from' motivation doesn't feel good and there is the danger that when you focus on what you don't want (i.e., not being alone), that's what you'll get. Remember Attitude 2: 'I create what I want').

The problem is that 'away from' motivation is not consistent. For example, if one of your values is 'not being alone', you will take massive action to be with someone. Once you are with someone, your motivation drops and the relationship may suffer. In contrast, 'towards' values have much more consistent and long-term motivation. 'Away from' values are created during significant emotional experiences – for example, when we are left by a partner, we may create a new 'away from' value of not wanting to be alone. These are created at an unconscious level so we are not necessarily aware of them consciously until we work through a process like the one in this book. To change these you need to become consciously aware of them. As I've said already, awareness is a vital first step. Then ask yourself, as we've done before, what there is for you to learn from that 'away from' value. How is it specific to you, positive and for the future? This will make it easier to let the negative experience go.

● CASE HISTORY: **MY STORY**

Facing the inevitable

I met my ex-husband in 1985, when we were both on a management course. I was struck at first by his physique. He is very tall and was very athletic in those days. He was running a department of the local authority where we both worked and I was a seriously ambitious young manager. He was nearly 10 years older than me. When we married a few years later, I was 30 and he was almost 40. Our daughter arrived 9 months after we married. Having the children early in the marriage did put a strain on our lives. I continued to work full-time and he was becoming increasingly stressed in his role at work. Gradually life became all about the kids and work, leaving no space for our relationship. I was getting lots of promotions and soon became the main wage-earner, especially when I left local government to join one of the top global consulting firms. I was gearing up to success and he was winding down.

The clash of our values began to emerge, though we were in denial for a long time. My work as a consultant took me away a lot and I began to travel extensively and meet new and exciting people. He took the opportunity to retire early at 50, and became a househusband, as well as running a small holiday-let business. Looking back, that's when the serious issues emerged. He was tired from looking after two demanding children, especially when I was away for long periods of time, and I was tired from travelling

➤

extensively and working long hours. The cracks began
to show. I then got into NLP and started to ask myself
different questions about my relationship. At first
I thought it was worth saving, and worked hard to
communicate what I needed to my ex. I wanted more
relationship time, more excitement and more passion.
He paid lip service to this, but took little action. We
seemed to have less and less in common.

The crunch came in 2000 to 2001, when I did my
NLP Trainer's training. Life was never the same again for
me, and I began to feel that the relationship was beyond
saving. We seemed to be on such different journeys.
I did my best to articulate and demonstrate what
needed to change. On New Year's Eve 2001, I gave
him an ultimatum: if things did not improve by Easter, I
would move out. Easter came and nothing had changed.
I took the impossibly tough decision to move out of the
family home, and to make a new home for myself and
my children.

My marriage and the other relationships I've had since
have helped me to become very aware of my own personal-
relationship values. My list helps me to sieve very quickly
through the men I now meet and it allows me to press 'delete' and move on if my values are clearly not going to be
met with that person. I am happy to be single at the moment, knowing that when I make a choice it will be the right
one – and a decision for life.

The secret weapon of your 'deep love strategy'

What many people don't realise is that in addition to our relationship values we also run something called our 'deep love strategy' (DLS). This is what keeps us secure in a long-term relationship, as it's what our partner needs to do for us so we know that we are deeply loved. If our partner isn't fulfilling this strategy, we may start to feel insecure and may even be tempted to replace them with someone who does!

In a brand-new relationship, both parties work hard to do everything they know is important to their partner, from taking them out, cuddling them on the sofa, telling them that they love them and so on. But, after a while, life settles down and couples revert to type. They use their own DLS with their partner, because this is the strategy that reflects what *they* want. If both partners have the same DLS, then they are more likely to continue satisfying each other. But if their strategies are different, both partners are likely to become dissatisfied with the relationship.

● CASE HISTORY: **MY STORY**
Please do it for me
The first time I discovered 'deep love strategies', so many things fell into place for me. Before then, when I talked to my husband about doing things for 'the relationship' I meant having surprises, such as being taken away for a passionate weekend or to a very

special restaurant – or being bought something special. I loved those things, as they kept the relationship alive for me. However, he rarely did any of these things for me, for us. In the end I began to arrange for him the kinds of surprises I would love to have, in the hope that he would get the hint and start to do them for me in return. I used to become frustrated when he didn't seem to appreciate any of my special 'treats'.

In contrast, he preferred a quiet night in with a good bottle of wine and a cuddle on the sofa. I thought that was boring! This went on for years, with me becoming increasingly resentful of what he wasn't doing for me. In the end, I gave up the special treats and surprises for him as nothing much came back in return. Towards the end of our marriage I learned about 'deep love strategies'. Sadly, although it didn't save our marriage, it helped me understand some of my frustration with him. My DLS is a visual one, so I needed him to surprise me and look at me in a certain way. His strategy is a 'feelings' one (or 'kinaesthetic' in NLP terms; see page 61) and he needed me to be more 'touchy-feely' with him, and enjoy those moments of closeness instead of wishing I was somewhere more exciting.

The challenge is to bring our DLS to the surface so we can act on it. I am going to show you how to make this important discovery so that you can share your strategy with your partner, and they can share theirs with you.

● EXERCISE 19
My deep love strategy

Ask yourself this question and make a choice between the three answers. You must choose one even if you like them all. One will be a stronger preference for you. (In NLP terms, these strategies are a reflection of our preferred communication styles, be it visual, auditory or kinaesthetic; see page 61).

The question is: 'In order for you to know that someone deeply loves you, is it absolutely necessary for you to:

1. be bought things, taken places or be looked at in a particular way? (Visual)
2. hear a particular tone of voice or certain words? (Auditory)
3. be touched or held in a particular way or place? (Kinaesthetic)

My answer is:

....

So now you have your DLS. For those of you in a relationship, go and ask your partner the same question and work out what you need to change (if anything) to ensure you are both fulfilling each other's deep love strategies. This will have an important role to play in the long-term success of your relationship.

➤

> Recently, I was chatting to one of my students, who discovered to her horror that she had spent 20 years with her husband, fulfilling her own DLS instead of his. His was visual and hers kinaesthetic – the opposite of the challenge I had with my ex. She had been blissfully ignorant of this and he had always been too polite to mention it. Now they've had the conversation and are fulfilling each other's strategies, the chemistry between them is greater than it has ever been.

Values in other areas of our life

I've taken you through the process of eliciting your relationship values, so now it's time to explore other key areas of your life – such as your career. The process is exactly the same. Elicit your values, put them into a hierarchy and then score each out of 10 – depending upon how well your current job comes up to scratch.

If there is a big gap in some areas then you may need to ask yourself a couple of questions:

- Without changing your job or career, can you make alterations to what you currently do so that it meets your values more closely? For example, if one of your values is variety and you are in a routine job, can you ask your manager if you can do some new work?

- If this is not possible, is there another career that you should consider? For example, if one of your values is 'contact with customers', but your job is a desk job that requires no contact with the outside world, maybe it's time for you to consider moving into a career that would involve dealing with customers on a daily basis.

In my experience, it is better with relationships *and* careers to ask yourself first if you can make the current one work. If not, only then should you consider moving on.

I am true to myself

This chapter has taught you how to be true to yourself, even if that means disappointing others in the process. It is so important that your relationships, job and everything else in your life is what you want, and not what you feel you have to have. Only then can you be who you really are. As I've shown you, many women sacrifice what's important to them for a life in the Grey Zone – with the wrong person, in the wrong career, with the wrong friends, living in the wrong place, and so on. They bite their tongues and keep their views to themselves in order to have a quiet life. There's no excuse for living like that any more! You are now aware of what is most important to you, enabling you – once and for all – to take responsibility for everything that is in your life. Things no longer happen *to* you – you're in control – and before you know it you'll be heading for the Brilliant zone!

I've selected a few lines from my favourite poem by Oriah Mountain Dreamer because they summarise the whole ethos of this Attitude.

From 'The Invitation':

It doesn't interest me if the story you are telling me
is true.
I want to know if you can
disappoint another
to be true to yourself.
If you can bear the accusation of betrayal
and not betray your own soul.
If you can be faithless
and therefore trustworthy.

**You can use values as a powerful tool in everyday
life. If you want to find out why people do things,
ask them the elicitation question: 'What's
important to you about ... ?'**

ATTITUDE 5

I Am Good Enough

F or many midlife women, believing in themselves can be their biggest challenge. Our beliefs act as an on/off switch in our brains. If we believe something is possible for us, we will act on it and get the result we want. If we don't, then we won't. Or, if we do act, we are likely to be rather half-hearted about it or even sabotage our success. Critically, our potential achievements will be diluted if we do not believe we deserve them, or we do not believe we are capable of achieving them – whatever 'they' are. We call these 'limiting beliefs'.

For example, you may have a goal of starting your own business, so you study hard to develop the skills and abilities to enable you to do it well. You visualise that goal every day. You imagine what it will be like – what you will see, hear and feel inside when you have achieved your goal. Yet, if you also have a little voice in your head telling you that you'll never be good enough to achieve that dream, you are unlikely ever to get going. And if you do get started, you will give up at the first hurdle.

In this Attitude we are going to explore how to change these limiting beliefs or fixed ideas that we have about ourselves. Everyone has them; the good news is that they can be changed!

Writing our own scripts

So what are beliefs? Our beliefs are views or ideas we have about ourselves, other people and situations that we hold to be true. Like our values, our beliefs are formed during the imprint period, before the age of 7. We collect beliefs from those closest to us at that time, such as parents, teachers, church leaders, close family, and any other important people in our lives. I told you earlier that I was brought up in the East End of London in the 1960s and 70s in a working-class community – a time when some of the community beliefs stemmed from life being hard and money scarce. Because of this, families stuck together and our neighbours looked out for each other. Even now my parents and sister live close by me, though we no longer live in London. When I struck out and moved out of London in the late 1990s, partly to escape the close ties of my family and to create a safer lifestyle for my children, it took less than five years for my family to follow! My upbringing greatly influenced my beliefs about work and money, and limited my thinking about what was possible for me and my business for many years. Now all that has changed and I have stretched myself beyond my wildest expectations by changing everything in my 40s.

The most important thing to understand about beliefs is that they are generalisations that we create from life experiences. Most of us do not consciously decide what we believe. Furthermore, once we have a belief we forget that it can be changed, and it becomes our reality. Now that's scary. We rarely challenge our long-held beliefs and they become

● CASE HISTORY: **IRENE**

Taking the chance

One of my clients, Irene, had started to paint late in her life – at 45, to be exact. She had just lost her husband to cancer and, in the beginning, she started painting for therapeutic purposes. Her friends began offering to buy her paintings and even asking her for commissions. She loved painting and wondered if she could ever make a living from it. One of her friends offered to sponsor an exhibition for her to kick-start her new career. Irene was really excited about this, and the two of them planned an exhibition to take place 9 months later, which would allow her time to prepare enough work. She started off really enthusiastically, and got four paintings finished in the first three months. Then her motivation started to wane and she noticed herself making loads of excuses to prevent herself from working. Her relationship with her friend, who had invested heavily in the exhibition, was on the line.

Irene became more and more frustrated with herself, and came to see me in the hope of discovering what was going on. Irene's pattern was actually not that unusual. There were some limiting beliefs about herself lurking deep in her unconscious mind, which ended up sabotaging her. It turned out that when she was a child, her mother always put her down. She was the eldest of three kids, and her mother set very high expectations that she struggled to live up to. As an adult this manifested as an internal conflict between the part of her that believed she could paint well enough to have an exhibition and

➤

the part of her that was her mother's voice nagging in her head about being a failure.

Irene had no idea that these battles were going on in her head unconsciously. Awareness is the first step. We then worked on changing her limiting beliefs and she left feeling very positive about her future. She was totally inspired and now believed she could do it.

I went to the exhibition. It was packed and most of the paintings had red stickers on them indicating that they were already sold.

a filter through which we sieve all of our life's expectations and experiences. So, if I don't believe I'm good enough, then I filter all my experiences through that belief until I only notice the times this is true. I don't notice all the times I was successful, or even *more* than good enough. Does this resonate with you at all?

Sometimes one careless comment from our parents can shape what we (unconsciously) decide is possible for us for the rest of our lives. For example, if a parent tells his or her child that they are stupid or ugly, or that they looked fat in a particular outfit, it can have a lifelong impact.

Our parents did the best they could with the resources they had, so this is not a time for recriminations. What they didn't know at the time was that even a throwaway and seemingly 'harmless' comment can do untold damage. Why? Because it can go straight into our brain, where it becomes stored as a limiting belief. I'm sure that if people realised this they would be so much more careful about what they say to their children. When I learned about NLP, I remember cringing over some of the things I'd said to my two wonderful children when they were tiny. The important thing is that once we learn how beliefs are formed, we have the opportunity to change them and break the negative patterns of our past.

The change model

When we want to make a change in our lives, we have to move from where we are right now (i.e., the present) to where we want to get to (i.e., the future). We are supported by our empowering beliefs and we are held back by our limiting beliefs. This often feels like a battle going on inside our heads. One voice is telling you to go for it, and another is freaking you out by asking you who do you think you are! For example, when I set up The Change Corporation, I was supported by my empowering beliefs as a trainer. I knew that I was a good trainer from the feedback I had been getting over the years. However, my limiting beliefs about my ability to run a business were holding me back. I had no one to guide me and I've learned the hard way through my mistakes. And, there have been many of those! Now I believe I am on the way to becoming a good businesswoman who will only get better. So our beliefs can change over time – that's the good thing.

It never ceases to amaze me how our adult lives are influenced by beliefs created during our childhoods, and often not even consciously remembered. I've lost count of the clients who have in some way been negatively influenced by a throwaway comment made by parents and teachers (who knew no better) that have lasted all their lives. I wonder what your beliefs are about you?

● CASE HISTORY: **KAY**

Never good enough

Kay was the younger of two daughters and had always lived in the shadow of her bright and attractive sister. Throughout her schooling she was constantly compared to her sister and she usually came out a poor second. She left school at 16 after getting some decent GCSE grades and joined the public sector, working in London as an administrator. She enjoyed her job, as it offered her the opportunity to prove herself. Slowly and deliberately, she worked her way up through the ranks until she ran a busy general office. Life working in London was tough, as she now had a young family of three boys, and was always battling to get to work on time and to fulfil all her family and work responsibilities. Things ticked along until she got a new female boss. This new boss began to give Kay a hard time for reasons she never understood. Nothing she did was ever good enough. Although she didn't realise it at the time, this situation had triggered negative emotions from Kay's past school life, which had been repressed for many years. The situation got progressively worse and Kay's health suffered. She contracted stress-induced asthma, and, at 42, she received an ill-health retirement and found herself without work, ill, and with her confidence at an all-time low.

When she came to see me, Kay was in a pretty bad way. These experiences throughout her life had shaped her beliefs about herself. She felt that she wasn't good enough to do anything and her self-esteem was at rock

➤

bottom. She also allowed herself to be put upon at home by her husband and three demanding boys. She wasn't able to achieve what she wanted in her life, as her needs always took second place. I helped her to make the connections between her early childhood and the situation with her boss.

Kay's low self-esteem and negative beliefs about herself had begun when she was a toddler. Her mother had constantly compared her with her older sister, who had a string of accomplishments to her name. The comparisons led Kay to believe that she simply wasn't good enough, and it created a pattern that played out throughout her life. Coming up against her complaining boss reinforced these beliefs. When I met Kay, we worked on her limiting belief of being 'worthless'. The first step for her was awareness, as most people are totally unaware of the beliefs and related patterns that they run. The next step was to help her to change her beliefs using the exercises in this book. She left feeling much more positive about her future. Her health is much improved and she now works locally. She continues to do well with her new company and she has recently become an NLP practitioner, which has boosted her confidence and assertiveness both at work and at home.

My role was to assist Kay in noticing the patterns she was playing out in her life. She began to understand consciously why she reacted the way she did. She now has more choices about how to live her life in future.

Changing our scripts

....

We can take steps to change our beliefs and I'm going to show you how to do this. We're going to start by noting both the limiting and empowering beliefs you've noticed about yourself. If you're not sure how to get started, think about areas in your life where you are not yet getting the results you want. If you don't yet have the results you want, there will be limiting beliefs that are holding you back. What do you think they are? What are the recurring patterns you've noticed in your life so far? For example, if you want to learn a new skill, why haven't you achieved that yet? Maybe you believe that you're not good enough. Or if you're not yet in a successful relationship, why aren't you? What has stopped you? Maybe you have the belief that men will always let you down. If you're still not sure about your own limiting beliefs, ask yourself what types of limiting beliefs your parents hold or held – are they also true for you? Ask your friends what they notice about your personal beliefs. Gather as much evidence as you can.

● **EXERCISE 20**
My beliefs

STEP 1: MY LIMITING BELIEFS
Examples of limiting beliefs include:

● Negations – e.g., I'm not capable, I can't make money, I'm too old, etc.
● Comparatives – e.g., I'm not good enough

➤

- Generalisations – e.g., Men always let me down
- All beliefs – e.g., I don't believe I can do it

Now, write down your own disempowering beliefs:

....

....

....

STEP 2: MY EMPOWERING BELIEFS

Examples of empowering beliefs include:

- I'm good at what I do
- People like me
- I'm a confident person

Next, consider areas where you are getting the results you want. What empowering beliefs are helping you to achieve that? For example, if you have lots of great friendships, maybe that's because you believe you are patient, generous and a good listener. You get the idea. Don't worry if what you write is not quite spot on; just brainstorm with yourself for now.

Now, write down your empowering beliefs:

....

....

....

➤

STEP 3: MY THREE MOST EMPOWERING BELIEFS

Choose your three most empowering beliefs and, for a week, keep a record of all those occasions when those specific beliefs have enabled you to move forwards. For example, if you circled a belief such as 'I can make new friends easily', observe the times when you have approached someone new to build rapport. Notice how good that felt and how often you did this. I bet your empowering beliefs are more active in your life than you realised.

STEP 4: MY THREE MOST LIMITING BELIEFS

Next, circle your three most limiting beliefs and ask yourself the cost of failing to let go of these beliefs, in terms of your goals. In other words, if you don't let them go, how will your goals be compromised? Write down the answers below, and be honest with yourself.

....

....

....

....

That wasn't pleasant was it? It wasn't meant to be. If we associate enough pain with a situation it often provides the 'tipping point', or impetus, for change. You may find that your limiting beliefs have already begun to be shaken up just by being aware of them and recognising the negative impact they have on your life.

➤

STEP 5: CHANGING YOUR LIMITING BELIEFS

We are going to work with each of your limiting beliefs in turn.

Take your first limiting belief – e.g., 'I'll never have a successful relationship'. As you think about that belief, notice the image you create in your mind. Notice what you see, hear and feel. Play around with the image by turning down the brightness of the picture, moving it further away from you, turning down the volume of any sounds and making any feelings less intense. Sounds weird, I know, but our brains can do this easily!

Then ask yourself: what's the opposite of that limiting belief? In this case it is 'I will have a successful relationship'. As you think about having a successful relationship, notice the image you create in your mind. Notice what you see, hear and feel. This time really ramp up your senses and especially your feelings. Make the picture brighter, the sounds louder and the feelings stronger. You'll know you're doing this right when you start to feel good about this idea. Now we are ready to start:

1. Get back the image in your mind that you will never have a successful relationship.

2. Now, replace it with the image that you *will* have a successful relationship. Make this image even more compelling each time you access it. Really go for it!

3. Continue doing this until you can no longer access the first image – all you have clearly in your mind is the new empowering image of you in a successful relationship.

➤

At first, you may find that you can get the idea of the limiting belief very easily, though the idea of the opposite or more positive idea may take longer. That's fine. As you as soon turn up the brightness, sounds and feelings, the intensity will change. Even if yo u can only get the opposite or positive ideal briefly at first, it is fine. You will notice that it becomes easier as the old limiting belief fades away. Once the old belief starts to fade away you know you are close to being finished. Keep going until it disappears completely.

Now ask yourself how you feel about that old limiting belief. Do the same for your other limiting beliefs and notice them freeing up and moving out of your system.

Well done! Keep focusing on your new empowering beliefs and you will be surprised how you begin to experience the world in a more positive and empowered way.

Reframing

Has anyone ever said anything to you that completely changed your perspective on an important issue? Sometimes people say things that absolutely change the meaning or the context of a limiting thought. In NLP, we call this reframing. In an instant it can change our beliefs forever.

Reframing is a brilliant NLP tool as it literally 'jolts' us into noticing something that we were not aware of before. In June's case (see opposite), linking the clean rug with her family not being around was enough to encourage her to start behaving differently. Although she still enjoyed a tidy

● CASE HISTORY: **JUNE**
Cleaning her family away

June was in her mid-40s when her family persuaded her to come and see me. She was obsessive about housework and it seemed to me that she had a mild form of OCD, or obsessive-compulsive disorder. Her family was fed up with her cleaning habits. She hoovered and cleaned the house at least 6 times a day. Her family called her the 'clean freak'. She was making their lives a misery, as she would clean up around them. None of them felt that they could bring friends home in case she embarrassed herself in front of them by cleaning them, too! Bringing her to me was a last resort. I remembered reading about a similar case written up by Richard Bandler (one of the creators of NLP) and I decided to use a similar approach.

I asked June to imagine her house all sparkly and clean. She was relaxed and very happy at that thought. Then came the important reframe. I said to her: 'And realise that means you are living alone and the people you care for most are nowhere around'. She became very upset at this point. In that instant the reframe had changed her belief about the situation. Then I got her to put some mess back in the house and know that her family was around her. Then she felt better again and the problem was resolved. The meaning of the tidy house was 'reframed' and it changed her feelings about it. Although she still likes to keep a tidy house, the obsessive behaviour improved dramatically and her family are all much happier as a result.

house, she felt better inside herself when she saw the rug had marks on it knowing that her family were around her!

Building self-esteem

Let's discover how to reinforce the new beliefs we have about ourselves by building our personal self-esteem.

People with higher levels of self-esteem feel comfortable in their own skin. They are relaxed about showing others their true self. Think about it for a moment. If you value and respect yourself you will naturally believe there is a lot for others to like within you. According to psychologists, our self-esteem reflects our overall evaluation or appraisal of our own self-worth. Our levels of self-esteem at any given point in time will be impacted and affected by our beliefs about ourselves. So it figures that if our beliefs change, our levels of self-esteem will also change.

We have worked on our beliefs and now we're going to re-inforce these changes by strengthening our self-esteem. Every word, image or emotion to which we are exposed over a period of time will either lower or develop our levels of self-esteem.

● **EXERCISE 21**
Growing your self-esteem

Self-esteem flourishes when it receives regular nourish-ment. This exercise will teach you how to feed your self-esteem to ensure that it continues to grow. It is

---

important that you select only positive qualities as you go through the steps.

Step 1: Remember a time when you were a child that you felt really good about yourself. What three qualities did you most admire about yourself back then?

1. ....
2. ....
3. ....

Step 2: What three qualities do you most admire about yourself now?

1. ....
2. ....
3. ....

Step 3: Imagine a time in the future when you have achieved everything that you ever wanted to achieve. What three things do you most admire about yourself at that point in time?

1. ....
2. ....
3. ....

Step 4: Think about a person who loves you. What three qualities do they admire most about you?

1. ....
2. ....
3. ....

Step 5: Think about a colleague at work who respects you. What three qualities do you think they admire most about you?

1. ....
2. ....
3. ....

Step 6: Take all the 15 words that comprise your answers, write them on a large piece of paper, and hang them somewhere where you can see them every day.

FINAL STEP: ANCHORING THE GREAT FEELING
As you look at each of the 15 words, notice how differently you are feeling. Notice *where* you are feeling each feeling. Spread the feeling throughout the rest of your body so it flows outwards and upwards. Do this each time you look at your list of 15 words. Notice how good it feels. Each day, as you practise spreading the feeling throughout your body, create a powerful anchor

for yourself by pressing together your thumb and fore-finger for around 5 to 15 seconds, as you experience the feelings at their strongest. As the feeling ebbs away, release your finger and thumb.

Do this every day when you look at your words. You will start to notice that by pressing your thumb and finger together you can access those amazing feelings about yourself. You can use this in any situation where you'd like to be in a more positive state of mind, such as before a presentation or an awkward conversation. For example, one of my clients with low self-esteem wanted to make new friends. She enjoyed dancing and joined a local salsa class. She felt anxious at the thought of walking into the dance hall by herself. I taught her how to use her anchor the moment before she opened the door. The positive impact of her anchor was enough to get her through the door and into the dance hall.

Developing personal charisma

Self-esteem is one of the internal drivers of charisma. Developing a stronger charisma will also help to reinforce your new empowering beliefs. What can we learn from women who project high levels of charisma? What do we notice about them that is different from other women? They tend to have a strong driving force in their lives, whether it's their career, family or partner. They also know where they are going, so they have a vision, goals and a direction in mind to get there. They also have high levels of positive energy and open body posture. You might say that they have an infectious personality that exudes confidence and charisma. Most importantly, they have a strong self-confidence and self-esteem, so that even when they make mistakes or they are challenged, they keep going and learn from that experience so they are able to do even better next time.

Who are some of the female icons today who have or had strong confidence and self-belief? Women like Joanna Lumley, Indira Ghandi and Michelle Obama have or had a magnetism, presence and self-belief that can be replicated.

A study led by British Professor Richard Wiseman explored how to become more charismatic. He found that 50 per cent of charisma is innate and 50 per cent is trained – so there's hope for us all. He came up with some ideas about how to become more charismatic:

- **Step 1:** Have an open body posture, hands away from face when talking; stand up straight, relax, hands at your sides. You should also keep your body balanced as if you were standing on a pair of scales – both halves should weigh the same. This will help you to appear 'grounded'.

- **Step 2:** When speaking to another person, let them know they matter and that you enjoy being around them; develop a genuine smile, nod when they talk, briefly touch them on the upper arm and maintain eye contact.

- **Step 3:** When speaking to a group, be comfortable and lead; move around to appear enthusiastic, lean slightly forwards and look at all members of the group.

- **Step 4:** To give a message, move beyond the status quo and make a difference. Be controversial, new, simple and counter-intuitive.

- **Step 5:** To give a speech, be clear, fluent, forceful and articulate; evoke imagery, use an upbeat tempo, occasionally slow or pause for effect.

These are all behaviours we can adopt to begin to appear more confident and sure of ourselves. Our brains cannot tell the difference between that which is real and that which is imagined, so adopting these behaviours will give a clear message to your brain that you are becoming more confident. After a short while, these 'trained' behaviours will become natural. What's interesting is that women do not need to be slim and beautiful to exude these characteristics. Anyone can develop personal charisma.

For example, Dawn French, born in 1957, has become the self-appointed champion of large women everywhere. Her mantra is that big women are not just sexy but are, in fact, sexier than their skinny counterparts. Despite some challenges in her marriage to Lenny Henry, she continues to appear comfortable in her own skin. Her autobiography, *Dear Fatty*, was a self-deprecating joke about her own size. She wrote that her confidence and self-belief stems from her father, who told her how beautiful she was each day. She wrote: 'He taught me to value myself. He told me that I was beautiful and the most precious thing in his life.'

When we take Dawn and examine what makes her so confident, we discover that she meets all of the criteria set out by Professor Wiseman. She is very open and relaxed – a warm and genuine communicator who makes physical contact with many of those she meets. She's also good in a group, as her high energy and passion shines through. She tends to be direct – even controversial – and has a clear and forceful way of speaking. Dawn is a great role model for all women, as she encourages us all to be proud of who we are and confident in our own skin.

● EXERCISE 22
Developing charisma

For the next week, I want you to think consciously about the way you carry yourself with others. Choose one of Professor Wiseman's areas and make a point of practising it. For example, perhaps you want to practise being more open and grounded with everyone you meet. By the end of the week, these techniques will start to feel more natural to you. In the following weeks, practise some of the other areas that are most relevant to you. As you continue to apply them in your everyday life, you won't even notice that you're acting differently. You'll be more charismatic, and positive things will begin happening to you before you know it!

I am good enough

What if your beliefs about yourself were in alignment with your goals? For example, if your goal is to start a new hobby and you believe that you can do it well, or if your goal is to lose weight and you believe it is possible. What difference would that make to you and the way you approach life? I guarantee that your journey towards your goals would suddenly feel very easy. You would soon begin to notice new opportunities that would have passed you by before and, for the first time in your life, your goals would become certainties rather than remote wishes.

Find somewhere quiet to relax. Close your eyes and imagine a point in the future when you totally believe in yourself. What will you look like, feel like and sound like when you truly believe in yourself? Now look back from that point in time to where you are at present. Notice how all the events between then and now can and will re-evaluate them in light of your new beliefs about yourself. It's totally possible! As soon as you take the first step forwards you will begin to reprogramme your future. Enjoy opening yourself up to infinite new possibilities and stretching yourself beyond what you thought was possible.

Notice how standing up for your beliefs builds self-confidence and self-esteem.

ATTITUDE 6

I Like Myself

Attitude 6 is about adopting a holistic approach to wellbeing. It will show you how to change your mindset so you can appreciate your body, eat healthily, age with grace and, finally, treat menopause as a new start – not the end of the road. Combined, these become the ultimate recipe for feeling great on the inside and, therefore, looking great on the outside. Imagine looking as amazing and feeling as healthy as someone in their 20s or 30s. This *is* achievable. The objective of this Attitude is for us all to feel good about ourselves and to be proud to look in the mirror and say: 'I like myself.'

Our affair with food

Let's face it – we women have an ongoing affair with food. We love it and we hate it. We starve ourselves and then we binge to make ourselves feel better. We go on crash diets and then we eat to suppress negative feelings in our lives. We equate it with love, yet we often simply feed others instead of telling them how much we love them. As the mother of a daughter who had an eating disorder at the age of 13, I know what it is to live with a fear of food and what it can do to someone you love. Food is a central theme in many women's lives so that's where we are going to start. We're going to explore what helps you create the mindset necessary for healthy eating, as this is the key to learning to respect yourself and feeling in harmony with your body.

The healthy midlife mindset

In Attitude 2: 'I create what I want', we learned about the power of our thoughts. We create our reality, so it's important to focus on what we want to achieve and create for ourselves. This is particularly crucial for women in the area of body image.

In 1999, a US study by Dr Jeffrey Hausdorff and Harvard graduate Becca Levy produced some surprising results: they discovered an unanticipated and powerful connection between unconscious perceptions about ageing and physical performance. For the study, 47 healthy men and women with an average age of 70 were randomly assigned to one of two groups. Individuals in each group played a 30-minute computer game that flashed words associated with ageing stereotypes on the screen. The words flashed by too quickly to read, but slowly enough to be perceived subconsciously. Those who received the subliminally delivered positive words, such as 'wise', 'astute', and 'accomplished', subsequently increased their walking speeds by 9 per cent. Those who received negative words about ageing, such as 'senile', 'dependent' and 'diseased', maintained the same walking speed.

Levy said: 'Individuals tend to acquire negative stereotypes about ageing as young as three ... When individuals become older, these stereotypes become relevant to themselves. Unlike stereotypes of race or sex, stereotypes of ageing become directly relevant to everyone who lives a normal lifespan. This latest study on gait demonstrates that the negative stereotypes of ageing that exist in our culture may have numerous implications for everyone who is already or who will one day become old.'

A later study by Levy reinforced her original findings. She found that age stereotypes internalised early in life can have a far-reaching effect on health. In a nutshell, those who held negative age stereotypes were significantly more likely to experience a cardiovascular event when older than their peers with positive age stereotypes.

Why is this relevant to me, you might ask? Well, it demonstrates the power of our unconscious thoughts on our bodies. We are continuously bombarded with ideas about our value, or lack of it, at midlife, and about the way an ideal female body should look. Our environment is always influencing our thoughts about being a woman – what we should and shouldn't do, and who we should and shouldn't become. What do you equate with being a midlife female? What views have you been conditioned to over the years that impact on what you believe to be possible for yourself? We know that ageism is active in our society – you only have to look at the media to find many examples of discriminatory behaviour.

So what damage are your current thoughts doing to your body? When you think you are not attractive enough, not smart enough, not slim enough or not strong enough, what effect is this having on you? What if these thoughts could be changed? What if, instead, you were to reframe your thoughts to being loved, beautiful, amazing, intelligent, resourceful and so on? How would that improve your love of yourself and, ultimately, your relationship with your body?

● CASE HISTORY: **NANCY**

Learning to love herself

Nancy had always struggled with her body image, which was mirrored in her battle with food. She is an outgoing woman in her late 40s; however, as a child, she didn't feel loved enough by her family. Her brother and sister were very gifted musically and Nancy was made to feel different and inferior for not having the same skills as her siblings. This caused her to become very unhappy with her own personal image. She didn't feel good enough about herself to eat healthy, nutritious food; in fact, she sometimes starved herself – almost as though she was trying to punish herself for not being good enough. At other times, she binged, because she felt so unloved and miserable. Her relationship with food was directly related to her self-image, and it was the cause of a vicious circle that led to a lifetime of yo-yo dieting and weight problems.

We worked together to reframe her beliefs about herself. I asked her to write out two lists of words that described what she thought about herself – one positive and one negative. The negative list was miles longer than the positive list, and many of her comments were to do with negative self-image. I helped her to understand how her long list of negatives had influenced her perception of herself and, consequently, her relationship with food. Using the techniques to turn negative belief statements into simple positive statements (we learned this process in Exercise 20; see page 154) such as 'I'm not lovable' to 'I'm loved and appreciated', she reframed her negative

➤

thoughts and repeated the positive thoughts to herself on a frequent basis. This simple method allowed her to start to take control of her thoughts and direct them towards the positive. As her self-respect grew she noticed that her view of her body image was also changing and, for the first time in her life, she was maintaining a steady weight.

So how do we create the right mindset to look after and respect our bodies? Firstly, we need to reframe the way we see our bodies. Instead of seeing them as less than perfect, or even ugly, it's essential to see them as the means through which we will achieve our life's purpose. We need to treat our bodies with love and respect, and regard food and meals as a way of providing them with the nourishment they require to support us on our journey. Any self-criticism will leave our bodies struggling to support us to be the best we can be. We must be ready to praise ourselves, and start being kind about every part of our bodies, knowing that any degrading thoughts will leave our bodies struggling. Our bodies give us the strength to achieve our goals and, in return, we need to truly love and respect them for the amazing tools that they are.

The necessary mindset can be found inside ourselves. It's not something we can get from an external source. We must start to believe in our own beauty and be proud of our bodies, and we must never be harsh or unfair in our criticism of ourselves. This is the best way of caring for ourselves and discovering the respectful enjoyment of food that we so desperately want for ourselves and our children.

Here is the mindset that every single midlife woman needs to embrace: ageing is a *positive* experience, and becoming older is something to celebrate rather than fear. Investing a little time in getting to grips with a healthier way of life can reap innumerable rewards — all of which will positively affect the way you look and feel. And when you look and feel great, anything is possible.

● **EXERCISE 23**
Growing to like ourselves

Step 1: List the negative thoughts that you have about your body. For example, 'I'm clumsy' or 'I don't look good in anything'.

....

....

Step 2: As we did in Exercise 20 (see page 154), take each of these negative thoughts and turn them into positive ones. For example, 'I'm clumsy' becomes 'I'm graceful', and 'I don't look good in anything' becomes 'I look great in whatever I wear'. List them below.

....

....

➤

Step 3: Rather like writing out lines at school, write down the positive thoughts or statements over and over, filling a page or two. Add your name to each statement. For example, 'Lindsey is graceful', and so on.

Step 4: Each day, stand in front of the mirror, looking into your own eyes, and repeat all of your positive thoughts or statements. Don't just say the words, though; repeat them until you feel that you are starting to believe what you're saying.

Notice how this simple exercise starts to have a powerful impact on your body image. You may find this a little uncomfortable at first. That's normal. Keep going with it.

Step 5: Finally, tell yourself each day about all of the things you have to be grateful for in your life.

It is our primary responsibility to find joy in ourselves because we will then transmit this joy to others. We women have a tendency to forget about ourselves in the process of nourishing and caring for those around us. We don't take enough time to care for ourselves, with our busy careers, the demands of parenting and looking after significant others. But if we don't find wellbeing in ourselves first, how are we going to teach our children and, in particular, our daughters, to live fulfilling lives? We are the models from which they learn and build their own experiences.

So, the next time you notice things you don't like about yourself, stop and reframe your thoughts into something positive. Over time, you'll get the hang of recognising negative thoughts (and perhaps be astonished by how often they pop into your head) and instantly changing the message you are sending to yourself. Start noticing the positives, too, and point these out to yourself as often as you can. Most importantly, treat yourself like you would a loved one – or your very best friend – and that means with kindness, affection and respect. You'll be amazed by how quickly you'll begin to feel good about yourself.

Fuelling up

There is more to optimum health and wellbeing than simply developing the right mindset about our bodies. It's also important that you realise the important role that eating the 'right' food plays in your life, and the powerful effect it can have on preventing disease. In contrast, eating the 'wrong' foods can have an equally devastating impact.

While finding and maintaining a healthy weight is important (and seems to be a constant obsession for many women), there are plenty of other reasons why a good, nutritious diet matters. For one thing, giving your body premium fuel will mean that it operates more efficiently. You'll have more energy (which is necessary for getting on with the plans you have for the rest of your life), your moods will be more stable, you'll sleep better and you'll suffer from fewer niggling health problems. Better still, you'll look and feel younger – and blast those ageing demons once and for all!

Before we go any further, let's look at your eating habits.

Be honest: are you really nourishing your body in the best way? Below you'll find a food diary, which I suggest you keep for at least a week, to get a true picture of what you consume on a daily basis.

● EXERCISE 24
My food diary

This diary should be used to record *everything* you eat and drink over 7 days. It is important to be totally honest with yourself. It's easy to 'forget' to add that second glass of wine, handful of cashews or second helping of pudding. However, you are only fooling yourself if you don't list everything that passes your lips – drinks included. Please complete the diary on pages 180–181 as accurately as you can – anything less than 100 per cent completion will sabotage the process of change.

HOW WELL ARE YOU EATING?

The point of this exercise is to get an overall snapshot of what you are eating and drinking, and when. You may be certain you have a pretty healthy diet, and then find that your food diary tells you otherwise! Maybe the 'odd' packet of crisps or gin and tonic is a little more regular than you had previously thought. You may find you are eating more than you thought; or even less. You may find that you snack a lot, or perhaps skip breakfast more often than you should.

➤

	Breakfast	Morning	Lunch
Day 1			
Day 2			
Day 3			
Day 4			
Day 5			
Day 6			
Day 7			

	Afternoon	Dinner	Evening
Day 1			
Day 2			
Day 3			
Day 4			
Day 5			
Day 6			
Day 7			

Underline the times when you are eating out of boredom, or for comfort. Have a look to see when processed food, takeaways or ready meals feature. Tot up the number of fruit and vegetable servings you manage in a day, too. I'm sure this will be an enlightening experience for you!

Make a note of any patterns or insights, and jot them down here.

....

....

....

....

....

Writing down what you eat and drink may be enough to encourage you to make the changes you need to create a healthier diet.

A healthy diet

Most of us are probably pretty clear about what constitutes a healthy diet, even if we don't always put it into practice. There are, however, a few pointers that are worth reiterating here – not just because they'll help you to look and feel your very best, but also because they are particularly important for midlife women. Why? Because eating healthy, nutritious foods increases vitality – that get-up-and-go part of the equation that helps you find the energy to meet your goals and achieve the life you want.

FRUIT AND VEGETABLES

Whether you are a vegetarian or a seasoned carnivore, these should form the bulk of your daily diet. You'd have to be from another planet not to have absorbed at least some of the hype, and in this case, it's spot on. Fruits and vegetables are literally bursting with vitamins and minerals that imbue good physical and emotional health. They also contain 'phytochemicals', which are plant chemicals that have some fairly miraculous effects on how our bodies and minds operate. Most of all, they include antioxidants, which are the 'anti-ageing' nutrients – they slow down the degenerative effects of ageing on virtually every part of your body. If you want to look and feel at your best, include as many different varieties of fruit and vegetables as you can. The more brightly coloured, the better!

WHOLEGRAINS

Wholegrains are effectively unrefined foods, such as whole wheat, barley, buckwheat, corn (including popcorn), quinoa,

Super soya

Soya is one of the best phytoestrogens (natural oestrogens) around, and can not only help to protect your heart and bones, but also reduce the symptoms of menopause significantly. Good sources of phytoestrogens include wholegrains, beans, nuts, seeds, berries, fruits and vegetables, but soya is the leader of the pack. Soya milk, tofu, soya beans – any form will help to encourage optimum health and wellbeing.

oats, brown and red rices, and wild rice. They contain lots of essential nutrients that protect against health problems, encourage healthy digestion (which means that what you eat is better assimilated by your body), and, perhaps most importantly, contain 'phytoestrogens', which are group of plant chemicals that can act like the hormone oestrogen – protecting your bones and heart, and even helping to balance your moods. Wholegrains are also low GI foods (in other words, they offer sustained energy throughout the day and won't make your blood sugar soar and then crash; see page 187), so they are a perfect part of the diet of any busy woman.

ESSENTIAL FATTY ACIDS (EFAS)

These are the omega oils that are contained in nuts, seeds and oily fish (such as mackerel and salmon), as well as some grains (such as quinoa), nut and seed oils, and even some vegetables, including broccoli and spinach. These oils are converted into substances that keep our blood thin, lower blood pressure, decrease inflammation, improve the function of our nervous and immune systems and – the bonus factor – improve mood and promote a healthy metabolism. They are essential for healthy skin (reducing fluid loss and supporting skin cells) and they also nourish the brain. Every midlife woman will benefit from EFAs, and lots of them!

PULSES

Beans, peas, chickpeas and lentils come from a family of vegetables called 'pulses', and are a very important part of a healthy diet. Not only are they a great source of healthy, complex (i.e., not refined) carbohydrates, which provide sustained energy throughout the day, but they are loaded with nutrients. Chickpeas, for example, contain nutrients

> Protein is required for the growth and development of healthy muscles, which burn fat. There is some convincing evidence that a high-protein diet can encourage healthy weight loss and stable blood sugar levels, with minimal cravings.

that are known to support the adrenal glands, which are responsible for our response to stress. Lentils contain plenty of iron, which is very important for midlife women, whose iron stores have begun to decline. In fact, if you are feeling chronically tired, iron deficiency may well be at the root. All pulses are a source of good-quality protein, too, which is absolutely essential in our diets. For example, protein is a component of every cell in the body (even our hair and nails are made primarily of protein), and our body uses protein to build and repair tissues, as well as make enzymes, hormones and other body chemicals. When your body begins to age, protein is even more important than ever, and pulses are one of the best sources around.

Making changes
Adding the foods known to enhance health and discourage the degenerative effects of ageing to your diet will change the way you look and feel in the short term; however, it's also important to remove the elements of your diet that may not be so good, in order to ensure health and wellbeing on all levels.

● So, begin by adding in all of the above – and let them form the backbone of your daily diet.

• Next, add a little good-quality lean meat. Meat provides the best source of iron, in the form that our bodies can most easily absorb. We need iron for energy, and several other body functions, too (including memory!).

• Dairy produce has had some pretty bad press over the past few years, but it remains the very best source of calcium, which midlife women need to maintain the health of their bones. So a little good-quality cheese, live yogurt, and low-fat milk should be a regular feature in your diet. If you find dairy products difficult to digest, try lactose-free milk or even goat's milk.

• Avoid refined foods, foods that contain unhealthy trans-fats (see page 189), white carbohydrates, such as white bread, cakes and biscuits, white sugar (choose honey, raw, unrefined cane sugar or maple syrup instead), fizzy or sweetened drinks, processed foods, crisps and other junk food, and anything that contains colouring, preservatives and sweeteners. I wouldn't expect you to lose the entire list from your daily diet, but if you can make a stab at limiting these foods, your health and energy levels will improve dramatically.

• Drink plenty of water. Water not only keeps your energy levels high by ensuring that every cell in the body is hydrated, but drinking regularly can also help improve your memory, your digestion, the health of your urinary tract and immune system, and virtually every other system in the body.

Sustained energy

When we eat food, its sugar is released into our bloodstream. Some foods, and in particular refined foods, such as cakes and biscuits, release their sugar quickly. This causes a surge of energy, followed by a 'crash'. There are a couple of reasons why this isn't a good idea. First of all, the rollercoaster ride of highs and lows can make you feel exhausted, and lead you to crave unhealthy foods to get a quick boost. You may find that you simply don't have enough energy to get things done how and when you want to, and the drops in blood sugar can also cause you to become moody and irritable. Secondly, foods that raise your blood sugar quickly prevent your body from breaking down previously stored fat, which causes the food you eat to be laid down as fat rather than used as energy.

There is a simple list that indicates whether a particular food is going to release sugars quickly or slowly, and this is known as the 'glycaemic index'. Glucose (which is basically pure sugar) is the fastest-releasing carbohydrate, so it is given a score of 100 on the glycaemic index and everything else is measured against it.

The simplest way to work out the glycaemic index of a particular food is to check one of the charts (you can find these on the internet, but see the box on the next page, which gives you a rough idea), which give foods a GI rating between 0 and 100. The higher the GI rating, the faster it will be digested. Simpler still, consider how refined it is. The more refined the food, the more quickly it will be digested, and the bigger its impact on your blood sugar levels. So, if it's highly refined, it's going to make your energy levels unstable, and it will probably make you fat. Go for foods that are in their most natural state, and base your diet around

Which GI?

GI foods fall into three rough categories:

- **Low:** 55 or less (desirable); foods in this group include wholegrains, most fruit and vegetables, pulses, dairy products, meat, eggs
- **Medium:** 56–69 (moderately desirable); foods in this group include honey, Basmati rice, baked potatoes, beans in tomato sauce
- **High:** 70 or more (undesirable); foods in this group include sugary cereals, processed foods, cakes, biscuits, white bread, chips, short-grain white rice

The more of the 'low' GI category you include in your diet, the more energy you'll have and the better you'll feel.

fibre-rich foods such as brown rice. Fibre slows down the release of sugars and gives them a lower GI; therefore, fresh fruit and vegetables, whole grains and pulses are all low GI.

Fat doesn't necessarily make you fat

As we've seen, some fats, known as 'essential fatty acids' or EFAs, are absolutely essential – as their name suggests. The more you have in your diet, the better you'll look and feel. And despite their bad press, some other fats are also essential for the smooth functioning of your body. These include monounsaturated fats, which are found in olive oil, vegetable oils, avocados, nuts and seeds. Saturated fats, found in animal products such as butter, cheese, fatty meats, whole milk, ice cream and cream, are a little harder on the body.

They are also found in some vegetable oils, such as coconut and palm. Eating too much of this type of fat puts you in an 'at risk' category for heart disease, high cholesterol and being overweight. Having said that, our bodies need some fat. About 35 per cent of your daily calories should come from fat – but no more than 7 per cent should be in the form of saturated fat.

The one type of fat that you should avoid completely is known as 'transfat', which is produced through hydrogenation – a process that makes an unsaturated fat (such as vegetable oil) solid or spreadable. This process changes the structure of fat, and makes it dangerous for health. Not only does it increase your risk of heart disease and stroke, but it is also implicated in a number of cancers, diabetes, immune dysfunction, and obesity and reproductive problems. Transfats are found in fried foods, commercial baked goods, processed foods, and more. Avoid anything with the word 'hydrogenated' on the label.

Does my diet really matter?

You may be at your perfect weight, and you may feel fighting fit and full of energy, but there is no doubt that improving your diet will have an impact on your health. What's more, it can improve your state of mind – because this Attitude is all about liking ourselves. When we like something, we treat it well. In this case, we need to treat our bodies in the best way possible. One of the most obvious and essential ways to do this is to change our diets so that we provide our bodies with what they need – foods that encourage health, steady energy levels, good mood and a balanced weight. Look at it this way: if you treat your body well, you are showing respect for yourself. I'm not a nutritionist, but there is sound science behind the need for a healthy diet, and I do know this: if you eat well, you'll feel good. And if you feel good about yourself, you will be capable of achieving almost anything. Self-respect is a fundamental part of self-belief, which underpins almost every Attitude in this book. If you take the time to show respect for your body by eating well, you'll be taking one more positive step towards achieving your goals.

Food and mood

One of the most irritating aspects of hitting the menopause is the plethora of symptoms some women experience. Mood swings and irritability are common, and can undermine even the most determined desire to make positive changes in your life. The good news is that eating well can not only help to bring these symptoms under control and keep your blood sugar levels steady, but healthy foods can also improve your mood! If you are in a good, positive mood, you will be much more likely to achieve your goals.

For example, EFAs have been shown to have a positive impact on moods, not only making you feel more emotionally balanced, but also encouraging the release of hormones and other brain chemicals that make you feel great. Similarly, healthy proteins, such as lean meat, fish, eggs, tofu, nuts and pulses, contain amino acids that make you feel more alert, positive and full of energy. In a nutshell, all healthy, whole foods will play a role in helping you to feel your best — both physically *and* mentally!

Choosing health

If you switch your mindset to choosing foods for health rather than thinness, weight loss usually follows naturally. This is especially true when combined with regular exercise and a feeling of respect and admiration for your body. These are common-sense strategies, and they are the *only* ones proven to work in the long-term. There is no ideal diet for everyone. The trick is to experiment with the right foods to find the right path to healthy eating *for you*. Last year, soon after my 50th birthday, I decided to change my diet and reduce the level of refined carbohydrates I was eating. As a result, I lost a stone and I've kept that weight off by permanently changing what I eat. I also feel much better for it and my energy levels are noticeably higher.

The truth is that trying to lose weight is unlikely to work in the long term; you'll likely end up feeling resentful and suffering from cravings that undermine your efforts. If you take a different tack, however, and simply change your diet in favour of healthy, energy-giving foods, you are taking positive steps towards looking and feeling great. This in itself will reap rewards that will keep you on track, and you'll reach a healthy weight as if by magic.

Defying the ageing process

There can be no question that we live in an appearance-obsessed society, and we are almost forced to draw comparisons between our bodies and the apparently perfect bodies of celebrities and models who dominate the media. Unwittingly, we begin assessing our bodies for areas that could be improved, and closely examine wrinkles, saggy bits, greying hair and even our basic physical shape. Not surprisingly,

> **Beauty sleep**
>
> There is probably nothing more crucial to a youthful, healthy appearance and a balanced, vigorous body and mind than deep, restful sleep. Aim for 8 hours a night, and make it *your* time, when the world fades into the distance and you relax into dreams of what will be!

many of us feel that we come up short, and that's where the problems begin. It's difficult to feel good about yourself if you think you are 'second-best' or 'faulty goods'. Equally, it's hard to be confident and present yourself to the world with panache and 'Attitude' when you have a niggling feeling that your lack of perfection is obvious to all.

Some women respond by hiding their bodies under baggy clothes or excess weight; others adopt a 'don't look at me' posture or body language that most certainly doesn't suggest confidence. Still others 'give up', and don't bother eating well, exercising or looking after their skin, because there seems absolutely no point. It's worth establishing right here, right now, that women who don't care for themselves appear, well, *careless*, and fail to exude the confidence and vitality they need to get where they want to be. What's more, failing to care for yourself sets you on a downward spiral – because if *you* don't think you matter enough to be treated well, who will?

At the extreme end, some women consider plastic surgery to iron out the imperfections – and not just signs of ageing either. Recent statistics indicate that breast enhancement and tummy tucks are up by 30 per cent, and that's a clear indication that more and more women are choosing a cosmetic procedure to help them feel better about themselves.

But guess what? Surgery rarely, if ever, does the trick. If you had issues before the surgery, you are likely to have them when you come out. Cosmetic surgery does not change your life. True, you may feel better about yourself for a while, but the feeling is not guaranteed to last.

● CASE HISTORY: SANDRA

An unsuccessful attempt to boost self-esteem

A friend of mine almost died at the age of 17 from anorexia, when she weighed just 5 stone (about 70lbs or 32kg). The anorexia was her way of controlling the negative feelings she had about herself. She recovered, though she continued to have self-esteem issues. Sandra is now 54. She had her first facelift at 42, and that kept her happy for a short while. Immediately after the procedure, she enjoyed the attention of family and friends telling her that she looked fantastic. However, within a year she was back to feeling depressed about herself again, and some of her old demons returned to haunt her. She was on medication for a while to calm her nerves. She is now planning her second facelift in an attempt to feel better about herself again. Sandra has never sorted out the cause of her eating disorder as a teenager – or the low self-esteem that has plagued her all her life. She refuses to work with a therapist – perhaps because she is fearful of what she may uncover about herself in the process. Sadly, her ghosts still haunt her and her second facelift is imminent.

This is a sad story that reinforces the fact that cosmetic surgery is not a 'fix' in itself. If you have emotional issues that create low self-esteem, they will still be there long after the surgery.

Weighing it up: risks vs rewards

It's important to understand that while some cosmetic surgery can bring short-term rewards, it will not change your life, your problems or your relationships. It is also important to understand that there is no such thing as physical 'perfection'.

Questions to ask yourself if you are considering cosmetic surgery include:

- Am I sure that I will get the results I want?
- Have I thought about the impact of any potential surgery on my friends? Will I be the subject of gossip when the operation is first done? If so, can I handle that?
- What if my partner exhibits signs of jealousy or insecurity because of my new and improved looks?
- (If it is a breast enlargement you are thinking of) Will I be totally comfortable with the increased attention I get with my newly enlarged breasts?
- What if I still feel 'ugly' or inadequate even after my 'problem' has been surgically corrected?

I would recommend caution, and trying other strategies before going under the knife. Evaluate the results you have achieved from these before going down the cosmetic surgery route. My best advice would be to use the techniques in this book, and particularly this Attitude, to change yourself permanently from the inside out. It's certainly a lot cheaper and safer than the alternative.

It's worth considering that a healthy lifestyle can be more effective at altering the parts of your appearance that leave you dissatisfied. For example, if you increase your intake of fruit, vegetables, wholegrains and good-quality proteins, your skin will improve, as will your energy levels and probably your weight as well. Getting more sleep can improve your mood, memory and even your appearance. Exercise is a given – toning and tightening can make a huge difference to the way you look and feel on every level. You may also find that natural, non-invasive treatments can help turn back the clock, and offer a short-term boost, without any risk of side-effects (not to mention little risk of unrealistic expectations). After all, a little pampering can go a long way towards helping you feel good about yourself.

You may wish to begin a good evening routine to look after your skin, and perhaps invest in a natural, youth-boosting moisturising cream. You may enjoy a massage, to iron out the stress that's making you tense and irritable. You may decide to take some supplements to keep your skin glowing and your hair strong and healthy. Unlike plastic surgery, which permanently changes the fundamental *you*, healthy, natural products and therapies will enhance the way you look, and encourage you to feel good in the process.

Learning to like yourself, and your body, is the healthiest thing that you can do, both emotionally and physically. Accepting who you are (and, of course, making the most of yourself) involves acquiring some self-respect. When you respect yourself, you treat yourself well, and exude a confidence and radiance that is not just appealing, but inspiring, too. A woman who likes herself and treats her body well will glow with good health and wellbeing, and be first through the door when opportunity knocks.

Menopause is the 'cure'

One of the biggest challenges we face as women at the mid-point of our lives is society's old-fashioned view of menopause as the 'beginning of the end'. We may be changing, but we must learn to embrace that change as opposed to mourning it and withdrawing. This is what I'm going to show you here.

> Aerobic exercise helps to increase the number of brain chemicals (called neurotransmitters), so that messages can be carried more quickly across brain cells. This increases mental flexibility and agility, improves concentration and alertness, and reduces the impact of stress. Exercise also increases the supply of oxygenated blood to your *whole* body, making you feel vital, energetic and glowing with good health. What's more, it encourages the release of 'feel good' hormones, which will lift your mood and help you to feel positive and energised.

First of all, there are many annoying and downright debilitating symptoms that can accompany menopause. Not all women experience all of the symptoms, but most experience at least some. This is not cause for celebration! The good news is, however, that by ensuring that you have a healthy diet, get some regular exercise and a good night's sleep, and have positive interactions and relationships in your life, your symptoms will be reduced. Furthermore, it's important to change your mindset.

Menopause spells *freedom* for most of us. Our child-bearing years are over, and with that, the frantic day-to-day activities involved in raising a family. Menopause isn't called 'the change' for nothing. It is a period of change that can spark change *in you*. The physical changes that you experience are accompanied by emotional changes that call your life to order. You can use this period of natural change as a springboard for being and doing exactly what you want. Women over 50 are just getting into their stride – and this year marks the beginning of the best years of your life.

Silver linings

My intention here is not to set myself up as any kind of expert on menopause, but rather to provide some basic facts about this important period of our lives. I'm in the 'perimenopause' stage myself, and have been experiencing the emotional turmoil of this state. The result is that I've been taking more risks, being more spontaneous and enjoying new experiences. I'm loving time on my own to make these discoveries, though I'm also very happy when my kids come back home again. I've often joked that if periods are called the 'curse' then maybe menopause should be called 'the cure'.

The menopause is a transition to a new 'season' in your life. It's not an illness or disease, and this is an important thing to note. Symptoms are simply evidence that all is changing; if you view them as something productive and positive – moving you out of what was perhaps a stagnant phase of your life and into something more fulfilling, challenging and rewarding, you'll be less likely to be dragged down by them.

There are a few ways to help you stay on track during meno-pause, and these include:

● **Deal with the symptoms.** If they are getting you down, then get some help. In other words, *take control* of your symptoms before they take control of you! There are many treatments, both natural and conventional, to help you cope with the symptoms you are experiencing. Don't be afraid to research them, talk to your doctor or even your friends, and actively seek out anything that will help you to feel more in control. You may decide that HRT is the answer; or you may go down the route of herbs, homeopathy, acupuncture or even reflexology. It doesn't matter what you choose; making an effort to get on top of unpleasant symptoms is a statement of sorts: you like yourself, and you want to feel the best you can. Taking charge of your health is empowering; suffering in silence is not.

● **Take care of yourself.** A healthy diet, regular exercise and relaxation techniques can actually improve meno-pausal symptoms. In addition, a healthy lifestyle will make you feel better about yourself because it reduces stress and encourages positive thinking and creativity. Even the worst day can be met and mastered with ease if you are feeling good about yourself. In Attitude 7: 'I take time for me', you will start to take a little time each day to focus on your own wellbeing. For now, however, treat your body as if you were a goddess.

● **Find support.** There is power – and comfort – in num-bers, and if you find other women who are experiencing the same symptoms and concerns that you are, you'll not only have a place to spill your emotional beans, but also a good source of alternative coping techniques. One word of warning: don't let a negative menopausal friend drag you down with horror stories or an apathetic 'we are finished' approach to life. Turn to other women to glean information, shed some worries and find a little inspiration.

- **Change your Attitude.** That's what this book is all about. You need to get on with your life, and ensure that it is going in the direction you want and need. Menopause is *not* an excuse to slow down. Your body is changing, so why not change the way you think as well? There is a certain power in this, because the options are all open to you, and you can choose the path you take into the unknown.

Midlife: the age of liberation

The menopause causes changes in brain chemistry that affect the way we think and process information. Because the temporal lobes in the brain are often more engaged, our intuition is enhanced. Some women also have more creative drive, as energy is focused on new areas. It's as if our bodies are telling us it's our turn now.

At the start of this book, I spoke about why 50 is a dangerous age for women, and that's something that's worth repeating here. For some, it's the time when marriage and children no longer hold the appeal they once did, and this is often combined with a heady cocktail of hormones that can make you feel restless. Many women walk out of long-term relationships in search of new excitement, and the glut

● CASE HISTORY: **KATIE**

Liberated from old ghosts

At 53, Katie left her 28-year marriage, which had been constraining for most of its duration. An early rebound relationship failed and, since then, she has been living alone. Her two children, aged 22 and 24, are largely absent, unless they want to borrow some money! Katie had wanted to travel for years, but her husband had never been interested. She had often thought about giving something back by volunteering in Africa, but she'd never had never had the confidence to do this while she was married. Once out of the relationship, she realised that she had allowed her husband to hold her back. Now, the only thing stopping her was herself. She had some money saved up, which she worked out would last her about 6 months – longer if she was living in a low-cost environment. So, Katie got in touch with several agencies and chose a project that set her up as a volunteer teacher in Ghana. In the end, she spent a year teaching young Ghanaian adults English, and had the most amazing experience of her whole life. She learned that she could do whatever she wanted, that it was never too late to change, and that she had unexpected qualities to share with others. At the time of writing she is back out in Ghana and having the time of her life.

of celebrity marriage breakdowns confirms that this is an unpredictable stage of life.

Women undergo a seismic hormonal shift between the ages of 45 and 55. A lower level of oestrogen means that we are no longer as concerned with mothering issues, such as keeping the peace and looking after our families. An increase in the hormone testosterone makes our more 'macho' characteristics, such as self-confidence, drive, determination and authority more dominant, and much more like a man's – and that can be very liberating.

This Attitude is about liking ourselves, and what better way to show this than to embrace the changes and let them take us to pastures new. It's a time to set new goals, and to put ourselves first, after years of little time for ourselves and our interests.

Midlife pleasures

There is nothing about menopause or perimenopause that inevitably decreases your sex drive or your pleasure in life. There are, without question, many things that affect sexual desire, including your physical and emotional health, being tired and lacking sleep, mood, relationship dynamics and even mobility. Some women find libido ebbs and flows according to their menstrual cycle, and changes again during and after menopause. Emotional issues, such as depression, anxiety and stress, can also put a dampener on desire. So taking charge of your health is the first step to getting your sex life going again. What's more, it will encourage you to feel great about yourself, and there's no aphrodisiac quite like self-confidence and enjoyment of your own body.

There is a certain freedom involved in sex during the menopause. For one thing, chances are you won't have to negotiate the slumbering body of a child in the same bed, the night wakenings by young children, and even the necessity of keeping the volume down. What's more, the threat of pregnancy will be diminished, and you can operate on a much more spontaneous basis. As a midlife woman, you'll know your own worth, and not be afraid to ask for what you want. There's no need to be shy – revel in your new approach to life, and welcome anything that brings you pleasure.

If you need more convincing, remember that a healthy sex life encourages the release of 'feel-good' hormones that keep you happy and positive. It also encourages stronger, more intimate relationships, which can provide a good foundation for a more exciting life. Studies have also proved conclusively that sex boosts your immune system, relieves stress, improves your cardiovascular health and, most importantly, improves your self-esteem. What's not to like?

● EXERCISE 25
Wake up to life!

Remember: passion, joy and fun begin in your mind. If you've not been having much pleasure in your life recently, or even if you have, use the exercise below to get started on enjoying your life more and more.

STEP 1: DO THE THINGS THAT GIVE YOU MOST PLEASURE IN YOUR LIFE
Make a list of the things that give you greatest delight – those activities that uplift and inspire you to keep going.

These are the special treats that make a real difference to you. For example, I love to buy myself a bunch of long-stemmed lilies every Saturday, as it gives me great pleasure to see and smell them each time I open my front door. Make a commitment to yourself about each one and how often you will indulge. Write your list, and how you aim to achieve it, below:

....

....

....

....

....

STEP 2: MAKE TIME FOR YOUR PARTNER (IF YOU HAVE ONE)

If your relationship has gone stale, or even if it hasn't, there are a number of things you can do to liven it up. First of all, remember the good old days. Why did you fall in love with this person? What qualities did you admire about them? Remember an event from the past when you were most happy with your partner. Imagine going back to that moment now. Run the event from start to finish in your mind and see, hear, feel, taste and smell all that occurred.

Keep running movies in your mind like this until you find yourself feeling differently about your partner. Invite them to play this game, too.

Write examples of amazing memories you share below:

....

....

....

....

....

Next, make sure that you arrange a date night (or whatever time you have available) on a regular basis. Go out together and enjoy different experiences. You can choose anything from a simple walk in the countryside to an expensive night out. Anything goes, as long as you are spending time together. Vary your activities, and notice that you begin to have more fun together again. If you still have young children, find a babysitter – your relationship is worth it. Write down ideas for your date night here:

....

....

....

....

....

STEP 3: DO SOMETHING DIFFERENT

Whether you have a partner or not, it's important to continue meeting new people and to keep on learning.

New experiences keep our brain cells healthy and alive. Think about those 'new things' you've talked about for years and not yet achieved. Now is the time. Here are a few ideas:

- Start a new activity, e.g., a sport, dancing, keep-fit classes, art classes
- Travel to somewhere new. If you are on your own, go with a friend or join a singles holiday
- Learn a new language
- Get back in touch with old friends; you can join Facebook or another social media site, or even start a daily blog so that they find you, and can keep tabs on what's going on in your life
- Learn a new skill, e.g., painting, cooking, photography, or even financial management
- Do some volunteering, e.g., volunteer hospital drivers, meals on wheels, reading with schoolchildren
- Join a new network or club
- Campaign for what you believe in

Write your own ideas below:

....

....

....

....

....

➤

STEP 4: CHANGE YOUR SURROUNDINGS

Start to spend more time outside, which has huge advantages for physical and emotional health. Taking a walk in nature every day is great exercise and can lift your spirits for the remainder of the day. Even repainting, changing the colour scheme in your home or office, or, at an extreme, moving house, can be a hugely positive exercise. Sometimes change to your physical environment can inspire the changes you need to make to the rest of your life. Just doing something *different* can have a positive impact as well; take a different bus journey to work, hit the shopping centre at the other end of town, spend a weekend in the country (or another city), or plan a day out doing something you've never done before. When you do things differently, you'll notice new things and all of this will spark your drive for change. Write your ideas below:

....

....

....

....

....

STEP 5: HAVE A MAKEOVER

Change something about yourself – maybe your make-up, your hair or the way that you dress. It doesn't have to be expensive. If you can't afford to go shopping, then invite

➤

some girlfriends round for a few drinks, and a 'makeover'. Suggest bringing along clothes they are willing to 'swap' and their favourite make-up and nail varnish. You can even simply arrange a little session to share ideas about how to give each other a different look. I added more colour to my wardrobe this year after getting feedback that I wore too many dark colours, especially black. I've enjoyed playing around with new ideas and I've had lots of positive comments. I've even noticed that I feel brighter when I'm wearing bright colours, which encourages me to wear them more often.

This may sound superficial and even a little trite, but putting some time into your appearance can reap rewards because it reinforces the idea that you like yourself – that you are *worth* the time it takes to make some changes. There is nothing more uplifting than a new look, even if it's a fantastic pair of shoes or a stunning new haircut. While changing your physical appearance will do nothing to change the way you feel about yourself on the *inside*, it can be an external manifestation of positive, confident thoughts. It can also be a little boost to get your self-confidence upward bound. Looking great tells the world that you care about *you* – and that you are someone worth liking.

My lifestyle goals

We've explored a range of wellbeing ideas in this Attitude, and now it's your turn to make a commitment to yourself about the changes you will make to your own lifestyle. Read back over this Attitude and decide what you are going to focus on. The idea is to encourage optimum health and well-being, so ideally you should set yourself some lifestyle goals that will have a positive impact. Perhaps you will decide to get some more sleep, deal with the stress in your life, eat a healthier diet, take some time to look after your skin, get some more fresh air, increase the pleasure in your life, get your sex life back on track, or get some regular exercise. Begin with the exercise on the right.

It is *never* too late

If you look in the mirror and *believe* that you'll never shift those pounds that are making you feel unhappy and less energetic; if you think that changes towards a healthier life-style are not worth considering because 'the damage has been done'; or, if you think that midlife is the time when you can sink into oblivion and let the world pass you by, you can think again! Ultimately, your life – both now and in the future – is firmly in your hands. If you think the worst, you'll get the worst. If you see your life and the life you *can* and *will* have with optimism and a sense of self-belief, you can achieve every goal you set for yourself.

Remember this: you are worth every bite of good, healthy food you put into your mouth, every step you take on the treadmill at the gym, every moment of good, restful sleep. You are worth treating with love and respect, because *you* are worthwhile. It is never too late to make changes towards wellbeing and every step you take will not just encourage optimum physical and emotional health now, but set you in good store for a happy, healthy future.

● EXERCISE 26
My new lifestyle goals

Choose things that you are really committed to changing or they will not happen. It's better to be realistic and pick changes you are committed to achieving rather than set yourself up for an inevitable knock-back when you don't achieve your unrealistic goals. For example, do not commit to going to the gym four nights a week if that is unlikely to happen. This is about widespread, lasting change, so set goals in all areas of your lifestyle.

● ....

● ....

● ....

● ....

● ....

● ....

● ....

I, ...

commit to make these changes from this date

....

Signed:

....

Growing older doesn't just have to mean 'getting old'; it also means moving forward in your life, and using all of the resources at your disposal to make this as seamless, happy and positive as possible. You aren't 'past' anything. Your life lies ahead of you in rich, glorious colour and if you stop right now and affirm to yourself that your future will be wonderful, you'll find the motivation you need to make positive changes to your life.

> **Look in the mirror and notice the real you. Tell yourself every day that you have never been emotionally stronger or physically more sexy and beautiful than you are right now!**

ATTITUDE 7

I Take Time for Me

One of the comments I hear most often from my midlife friends and clients is that they want more 'time for me'. What does that really mean? It means time to ourselves, to do whatever we want without having to worry about anything else, such as money or family responsibilities. This might mean shopping, a day at a spa, lunch or dinner with friends, or just plain chilling out. As midlife women it can be challenging to extricate ourselves from the daily grind to really enjoy the moment.

Two years ago, when my children were 19 and 16, I spent New Year's Eve with my two best girlfriends and stayed at one of their houses in London. I really appreciated leaving all my daily responsibilities behind, as I focused on enjoying my friends. Though my kids seemed fine about me going, my phone began to ring very early the next morning. I had calls from both of my children and my parents, who wanted (and almost demanded!) to know when I would be back. They had 'allowed' me my evening out; however, according to their model of the world, it was my responsibility to be back to sort out the food and entertainment for New Year's

Day! Neither of my two girlfriends have children, and I remember envying their laissez-faire attitudes.

As I was rushing around to get ready to travel the 100-odd miles back home, they were enjoying a leisurely breakfast and a girlie chat. I noticed how I put myself under pressure to get back home as soon as possible. It took the fun out of the morning for me, and I felt guilty all the way home! When I got back home, I discovered that no one had died and the family had found some food to eat. I had a strong realisation that I needed to start using time differently. Better still, I needed to take more time for me and to live in the moment!

● CASE HISTORY: **FOUR WOMEN**
Making time for themselves

I know a group of four women in their mid-40s, whose children are aged between 9 and 15. All of them have one child aged 15, because that's how they met – at the ante-natal classes before their first babies were born. During the early months, after the births, they made sure that they got together regularly. However, they did more than just have coffee together. They made a pact to give each other some space as their babies grew older. In the beginning, two of the mums would look after two of the babies while the other two mums popped out to the shops or for a cup of coffee. The only stipulation was that they had to get or do something for themselves and not their babies. As their children got older, the mums continued with this arrangement.

➤

When some of them went back to work, their get-togethers moved to the weekend – but the 'me time' arrangement stayed the same. As their children grew older, they were able to look after more children at a time, and when other babies arrived they were included in the arrangement. They now have seven children between them. Nowadays, the plan is a little more flexible, but essentially still the same – one of them looks after however many kids are around, while the other three go and do something nice together. They really look forward to this time without kids, and it has been a great way of creating 'me time' for all of them.

Perceptions about time

This Attitude is all about *time*. Do you embrace time as your friend or your enemy? Are you someone who often says, 'I don't have time for that'? If you are someone who experiences time as a scarce commodity, of which there is never enough, then you are creating a completely different personal reality from someone who perceives that they have all the time in the world. Your world is likely to be much more stressful. Maybe you have even experienced some of the symptoms of stress such as breathlessness, panic attacks and high blood pressure. Deepak Chopra, the world-famous Indian medical doctor and author, wrote of an Indian master, who explained his remarkably youthful appearance thus: 'Most people spend their lives either in the past or the future, but my life is supremely concentrated in the present.' This is because those who live in the past often suffer from guilt, and those who worry about the future often suffer from anxiety. However, if you live in the present you can focus on enjoying the moment, whatever you are doing. This has a more relaxing impact on the body.

When life is concentrated in the present, it is most real, because the past and future are not impinging upon it. Only *now* exists. If you can free yourself from the guilt of the past or anxiety about the future a space is opened for a completely new experience – the moment of *now*. The next exercise is designed to give you an experience of 'now' that is very likely to be outside of your normal 'time-controlled' way of being. It sets up an enjoyment of each moment that is likely to be much more intense and enjoyable – and at the same time, more calming – than you normally experience.

● **EXERCISE 27**
Living in the now

Choose a day when you are not pursuing your normal activities – maybe at the weekend or when you are away on holiday. Remove your watch and focus on putting all of your attention in the now. Enjoy every moment. It doesn't matter what you choose to do – it may be time with the kids, friends or your partner. Equally, you may choose to spend time on your own. Whatever you decide, the important thing is to give that activity, person or people your full attention. Play at 100 per cent. Take your awareness into the region of timelessness.

Notice how you experienced time in that situation. How did you feel? What happened? One of my NLP practitioner students did this exercise and found that it helped her to de-stress when she was back in 'normal work' situations as she was focusing less on the negative feelings of not doing something well in the past or the future. She focused on doing everything in the moment to the best of her ability. She became much calmer after practising this approach. Make a note of how you experienced it below:

....

....

....

....

....

....

....

Time is an illusion

One of Einstein's great contributions to modern physics was his theory that linear time is superficial. Time seems to pass, clocks tick off their seconds, minutes, hours, days – events come and pass. However, although this activity is relative to what you are doing at that time, it has no absolute value. You know yourself that time drags when you have chores to do, but if you were out for a romantic meal with your partner it suddenly speeds up!

Einstein was one of the first great challengers of time. He proved that there is no such thing as linear time (time can speed up or slow down, as the example of the romantic meal versus housework demonstrates), and he showed that the experience of time depends on the situation of the observer. So, when you are with the person you love, you experience time moving faster than at other moments. Quantum physicists suggest that there is no absolute past or future, either. In fact, there is an infinite number of probable pasts and an infinite number of probable futures for each of us. Everything that could have happened did. You chose what possibility to create for yourself using your 126 bits of data per second entering your nervous system via all your senses. The really exciting thing to realise is that we can only experience now; never the past or the future. Of course the past happened. And, when you think of a childhood memory, you are not experiencing the past but your perception of the past in the now. The same goes for the future. If you imagine an event in the future, you are experiencing your perception of that event now. You can't have a problem with your childhood, as that is past. You can, however, have a problem with your perception of it *now*.

This is exciting for us as we can change our perception of events, past or future, in the *now*. This is because we choose our thoughts and so we decide if we choose to feel miserable or happy about a past event in the *now*. This is a completely different way of considering time. There is no absolute time or absolute memory. We are dealing with our *perceptions* of time and events, which can be changed.

The attitude you take towards time says something about you. For example, if you live your life constantly putting yourself under huge time pressures, you are more likely to develop health-related problems associated with stress. Even the word 'deadline' sounds threatening, as it contains the word 'dead'. It implies that you're in real trouble if you don't deliver on time. My life as a business consultant was once like this. Every day had a deadline attached, as yet another client was waiting for yet another deliverable. My life then was very pressured. Now I decide when to pressure myself! One of the things I've personally noticed since leaving consulting is that my life is far less stressful than it was – and interestingly that's not about doing less work. It's much more about feeling in control of what I do and what I choose to take on board. My ex-colleagues comment upon how grounded and calm I look in contrast to their grey, ashen faces, as they dash about their lives as if the world is about to end if the client doesn't get their report on time. My old company had a bad habit of setting deadlines that were far too tough.

Have you ever experienced something similar? If the client said they wanted the work in a month, our guys would often respond with 'We can get it to you in two weeks'. It seemed to be some macho, egotistical way of creating pressure for those of us who then had to deliver. What can you do to relieve time pressures at work when you are not in control of your own time? You can begin to challenge the deadlines that are set around you to discover if they are 'artificial' or 'real'. You can also negotiate for 'more time'. I've also known many people who put many artificial pressures on themselves in their private lives, too.

● CASE HISTORY: **LINDA**

Modelling bad behaviour

Linda's mother used to put daily pressure on Linda and Linda's father, and this was something that Linda learned to model very well. Each day, there was a list of tasks to be completed, with pressure set from the word 'go' to get them all done on time. Linda's mother was disappointed if this 'artificial' timetable was not met. The list was 'artificial' in that rarely did any of the tasks 'have to' be completed that day and because there was always far too much on the list. The list was Linda's mother's unrealistic expectation of what she felt 'needed' to be done that day. Linda unconsciously modelled these behaviours for years, especially at the weekends. In her head she would tell herself all the things that must be done that weekend – or else! She would then rush around like a crazy thing until some of them were done – and then always felt bad if tasks were outstanding. If she had fun instead of doing her chores, she would feel guilty about it afterwards.

When she came to see me I went through all the items she regularly 'told' herself had to be finished and prioritised them with her. We spread some of them over a much longer period of time, we crossed some of them off the list as unimportant and some things we gave to others to do. I helped Linda realise that she had personal choice over her use of time. Now she lives life much more in the present. She takes more time out, and whatever she does in the moment she does at 100 per cent. What she doesn't get done waits until another day. And, most importantly, she now feels great about all the things she does achieve.

The power of meditation

Let's complete this section about changing our perception of time by learning about the power of meditation. Meditation is described as a state of timelessness achieved when you clear your mind of conscious thoughts. Deepak Chopra said: 'When this [meditation] becomes a reality, the fears associated with change disappear.'

Since meditation entered the mainstream Western world experience, scientists have applied measurements to the process. They discovered that the physiological state of people who meditate undergoes definite shifts towards more efficient functioning. For example, the hormonal imbalance known to speed up the ageing process is reversed. People who meditate in the long term can have a biological age that is 5 to 12 years younger than their chronological age. In other words, meditation alters the frame of reference that gives the person their experience of time.

This is even more evidence that we can manipulate time for our own benefit! Meditation is also a great way of 'taking time for me', as you can retreat into your own universe and spend time discovering the real you.

● **EXERCISE 28: MEDITATING ON ME**

Get yourself in a comfortable position. Sitting cross-legged is good position. Lying down and falling asleep is not meditation – you need to keep your awareness with you. Close your eyes and block out all thoughts, except the

➤

---

question about what's next for you in terms of your personal development. If you notice other thoughts coming into your mind (which you will in the beginning), find something to say to yourself that will get you back to the exercise. For example, I say to myself: 'talking, talking', which reminds me to empty my mind again and go back to the exercise. Pay attention to the thoughts that come into your mind when you meditate on this subject. Notice how you feel about them. Notice especially the thoughts that come up from an unconscious level. Meditate for at least 5 minutes, then extend it. Find a moment each day to mediate on what it is you want to achieve.

After the 5 minutes, use the space below to write down what came into your mind and how it helps you to decide what to do next:

....

....

....

....

....

....

Making the most of *now*

So what does this mean for you? We are only on this planet for a relatively short time, so it's important to use time as wisely as possible. Stop making excuses! You can create more time for you whenever and wherever you choose. Take control of time before it takes control of you. Truly make the most of every moment, and play it at 100 per cent. At midlife, we are halfway through our lives – maybe more than halfway for some. I'm 50, so I guess I'm more than at my halfway point. Therefore, let's use time as if every day is our best day. Too many people come to a point in their lives when they regret not doing what they really wanted to do. Remember that the experience you have always wanted to have may not be a possibility for you tomorrow. I recently took my mother to have her first manicure at the age of 77. That's a long time to wait to be pampered. Make sure that you do not put yourself in a similar situation. Think about what you want more of in your life. How can you create space for those things? What does taking 'time for me' really mean for you?

● EXERCISE 29
I take time for me

In the space below, make a list of all the things you want to make more time for in your life and how you will create more time for each of the items. The only rule is that they must be things or activities for you alone. For example, you might decide to go and enjoy a quiet coffee at the local coffee house on Saturday mornings while you read the paper, or go for a walk in the countryside on Sunday afternoons. They do not have to be expensive things; in fact, many of the most pleasurable activities can be done for free. Use this list as an action plan for what you want

➤

to create for yourself in the future. Commit to yourself a
timescale as well for each idea and stick to it!

- ....
  ....
- ....
  ....
- ....
  ....
- ....
  ....
- ....
  ....
- ....
  ....

Bringing it all together

By midlife, we have often created many poor habits around
the use of our time. We have allowed ourselves to be stretched
in far too many directions with little or no time left for ourselves. Use the following checklist to change your personal
experience of time:

- Challenge your personal perception of time. Start focusing on having enough time to do what you want. Life
  will immediately become less stressful! Live in the now

rather than in the past or the future. Stop wasting your energy on the past (too late!) or worrying about the future (too early!).

● Do what is important rather than what you perceive to be urgent by setting 'real' as opposed to artificial priorities.

● Create more time for what you want to do ... midlife is an important time to re-evaluate how you utilise time for you.

Financial strategies that work

Like it or not, we all have a relationship with money. How healthy is yours? I've included the theme of money in this Attitude for two reasons. Firstly, while there are many things in life we can do for free, if we are to have the time of our lives, we need to have enough money to do all of the things we want to do. Secondly, the two main excuses people use for not changing usually involve a lack of time and/or money. So the two are inextricably linked in the theme of personal change.

This section is going to explore where you are now in your relationship with money, and the reasons why you may not yet be accumulating the kind of money you would like in your life. We'll then look at top tips for you to build the level of financial capital you want. So whatever your financial situation, please read this section carefully, as I guarantee you will learn something important.

What do you believe about money?

Do you have the amount of money you want in your life? If you do, great! If you don't, it's vital that you read this section to discover why, and what you can do about it. The ability to have and keep money absolutely starts in the mind! Ask yourself if you have ever heard yourself say any of these statements, or if you believe them:

● You have to work hard to make money.
● Money is for other people. It's not for me.
● Money is hard to manage.
● It is difficult to make a lot of money.
● You need money to make money.
● Having money isn't spiritual.
● I'll never be rich!
● No matter what I do, I will never have enough money.

These thoughts/beliefs are driven by our unconscious patterning around money. I call them 'money viruses', and they prevent us from accumulating the wealth we want. We need to change our mindset about money before we can start to accumulate it. This requires reframing our mindset to believe that money will flow to us easily – and that it is inevitable. As you now know, if we focus our thoughts on negative beliefs, it's very likely that we'll end up attracting them to us. The first step, therefore, is to refocus your thoughts about money so that they become empowering beliefs, or the money viruses will get in the way.

The following exercise will begin to bring into your conscious awareness what you believe about money and will allow you to link that to your actual experience of money. For example, a client of mine who had major issues about not being able to make enough money discovered that she paid no attention to money – so it wasn't surprising that money paid no attention to her! It took the exercise below to draw this to her attention and it was a massive 'light-bulb' moment for her, which meant she immediately began to focus differently on money. She learned how to manage the accounts for her business and soon began to notice that her cost base was reduced considerably through her efforts, and that more money was starting to flow into the business through new clients.

● EXERCISE 30
Focus on what you want

STEP 1: OBSERVE YOUR THOUGHTS

In Exercise 11 (see page 63) we learned how to observe our thoughts. This time we are going to focus on our thoughts about money. Take a few moments now to let your mind and body relax a little. Reflect on your relationship with money up to this moment. Here are some questions to get you started:

- Has money been easy or hard to come by in your life so far?
- Have you been able to accumulate money or lose it?
- Are you solvent or in debt? How do you feel about that?
- Do you spend money to feel better about yourself?
- Do you have financial independence? If not, why not?
- What plan do you have for financial freedom in your life?

➤

Use the table below to jot down any other thoughts about money that are coming into your mind right now. Separate them into positive and negative thoughts and feelings, as we did before. Notice where the balance is — positive or negative.

Positive thoughts and feelings	Negative thoughts and feelings
....	....
....	....
....	....
....	....
....	....
....	....
....	....
....	....

STEP 2: AFFIRMATIONS

Here are a couple of short affirmations for you to focus on for 5 minutes every day. By focus, I mean find some quiet time for you. Relax and concentrate on these sentences; say them to yourself and shut out other distractions from your daily life. These affirmations will start to change the negative thoughts you may have had about money in the past:

➤

- It's easy for me to accumulate the money I want in my life.
- It's inevitable I will make the money I want in my life.

STEP 3: CHANGING YOUR BELIEFS ABOUT MONEY

We have already learned what a powerful role our beliefs play in our success. In the same way that we can never be more than we believe we can be, neither can we accumulate more money than we believe it's possible to have. It's important to recognise that your unconscious beliefs play a major role in your financial success – or lack of it.

For example, many people have an unconscious ceiling set on the amount of money they are going to have or to earn. Others had parents who taught them that to have money was wrong, or that it wasn't possible for people like them to have the money that they want. Our parents' limiting beliefs are then adopted as our own beliefs – on an unconscious level – and they become our reality, too. Ask yourself what your parents believe, or believed, about money. Did they have the money they wanted?

What impact did their beliefs and experiences have on your life? Use the powerful process of changing limiting beliefs that I taught you in Exercise 20 (see page 154) to specifically work on your beliefs about money or your money viruses.

● CASE HISTORY: **KATIE**

Sabotaging her own success

Katie came to see me because she just couldn't seem to make the money she wanted. It seemed as though as soon as she got herself on the right track, something would happen to sabotage her success. As I don't believe in coincidences, I was very curious about what she was creating in her life. For example, she told me about how she had made the big decision to leave her job as a department manager of a large supermarket to set up her own business from home, making speciality cakes. Yet, only two weeks into her new career she had broken her arm and found herself unable to work. This had obviously put financial pressure on her. She couldn't work out why she was unable to stabilise her finances to any degree. As soon as she accumulated some money, something negative always happened.

We discussed her past and her beliefs about money. When I discovered that her father had always worked hard and had ended up bankrupt, I knew that we were onto something. Katie was only 7 years old when her father went bankrupt. At that time, she formed an unconscious belief that if you work hard, you end up with nothing! It was a clear cause and effect in her 7-year-old unconscious mind. In fact, it set up a pattern of unconscious behaviour in her life that was to sabotage anything she worked hard to achieve. At an unconscious level, it was a self-preservation mechanism. In reality, of course, this doesn't make any sense. Hard

➤

work leads to bankruptcy only existed in her 'model of the world', which, of course, she had interpreted from her father's experience.

I helped her to understand that as soon as she started to work for something important, she unconsciously created an event that stopped her from (in her model of the world) becoming bankrupt. That accounted for her accident and the many times before when she had unconsciously created a negative event in her life. The connection was simple, really, and yet it had impacted her whole life. Katie was able to reframe her beliefs about money once she understood this. We worked on a new belief – that her monetary success was inevitable. Her cake-making business is now doing really well and she is extending her services to teach others.

Have you noticed that when you are truly congruent about achieving or getting something it comes to you easily? It is almost like the universe conspires to give it to you. When you are in conflict (especially unconscious conflict) or you are unclear about your goals, creating what you want is much more difficult. People who live abundantly do so because their beliefs about themselves and about life are in alignment with their goals. They also have a clear vision of what they want. So focus on what you want and align your beliefs. As a result, you will succeed with money.

Financial tips for women

We have come a long way in the equality stakes, but the odds are still stacked against us when it comes to financial matters. Despite the fact that we live longer than men, around 1 in 8 elderly women lives in poverty, compared to one in 12 men. Official figures show women are 14 per cent more likely than men to live in households with incomes that are 60 per cent below the national average. There is still a widespread assumption that women have men's income to fall back on, but this is out of touch with the lives of many women today and is one of the key reasons why women are more likely to face poverty than men. Government statistics show that almost half of all women have total individual incomes of less than £100 a week, compared with less than a fifth of men. Taking time out of work to bring up children, the high number of women in part-time or low-paid work, and the gap between women's and men's average pay all contribute to women's poverty.

Fortunately, there are steps you can take to improve your financial prospects and future. These work in alignment with the work we have just done on your beliefs about money. Now that you've sorted out the way you view money, here are some practical steps to help you get your finances on to a solid base for the future.

1. **Setting financial goals is the key to financial success.**
   Write down your financial goals on paper. Make sure they are SMART (specific, measurable, achievable, realistic and timed; see page 43). State the goal, when you want to get there and what you will do to make it happen. If you've always had trouble staying on a budget, develop a weekly or monthly spending plan.

2. **Spending less than you earn is the secret to accumulating wealth**. This is a simple fact that many of us pretend not to know. If you want to accumulate wealth, live below your means and invest what's left over.

3. **Money demands attention.** Money gets frittered away when it's not managed. Track your income and expenditure each month, rather than stuffing your bank statements away in a drawer without even looking at them. Reconciling everything you've spent each month against your bank accounts ensures that you know what your cash flow is at all times and you guard against any fraudulent payments.

4. **Deal with debt.** I'm amazed at the number of people I meet who stick their heads in the sand over debt. Open those bills, no matter how painful it is, and sort them out. Emotionally detach yourself from the debt – it's the sender's money, not yours. Negotiate with your creditors to pay back what you can. Focus on paying off your debts as fast as possible. Paying interest haemorrhages your chances of accumulating wealth. Set up monthly direct debit payments to avoid late payment charges.

5. **Do *not* use credit to live on.** Using credit to pay for day-to-day expenses like food shopping is one of the least smart things you can do, as it costs so much to repay. My 20–year-old daughter has the right idea – she does not own a credit card and saves for everything that she needs.

6. **Tidy lives equal tidy finances.** Those with cluttered lives often have cluttered finances, too. Take the time

to have a grand clear-out on all levels – your wardrobe, the house and your office. Tidy up everything and notice how de-cluttering your life will make de-cluttering your finances seem much easier.

7. **Education expands your mind and your earning potential.** As a rule, education brings a more interesting life and more money. Save some of that money and you can buy yourself financial freedom. Education is your ticket to more opportunities. Well done for buying this book. Now what's the next step?

8. **If you don't save when the opportunity is there, you will drown when it isn't!** Sooner or later you will need a cash cushion. Without it, your lifeline will be high-interest debt that will linger long after your problem has gone. For example, are you over-paying on your mortgage while interest rates are at an all-time low? If you could pay your mortgage before, make sure you use this as an opportunity to build a savings pot against your mortgage or reduce the interest you pay. This opportunity will not be there forever.

9. **Choosing a fiscally irresponsible partner is hazardous to your financial health.** Opposites tend to attract. Fiscally conservative women tend to be attracted to fiscally liberal guys and visa versa. If you're about to pair up with a big spender, don't sign up for any of his debt. If your potential partner is in debt, talk about how he or she will deal with their own debt, so you don't end up deeply in love *and* debt. One of my clients has just separated from her husband of 20 years. He has single-

handedly spent the £500,000 inheritance she had from her parents. Happily, she is finally free of him but, sadly, not free of debt.

10. **Train yourself to be financially independent.** If you plan on Prince Charming you may be in trouble, as all marriages end eventually in divorce or death and it's usually the women who are left behind. While women are the ones who handle most of the day-to-day finances, the majority of women leave the long-term financial planning to their partners. Mistake. Be aware of your finances even if your partner is handling the bulk of it. Get an idea of how much is coming in and going out, and where it's going. Check on the pension planning, too.

11. **Opt for long-term financial planning over crisis management.** Women do not tend to get serious about money until they lose a job, a spouse or are near to retirement. In her book, *Secrets of Six-Figure Women*, Barbara Stanny interviewed women earning very high salaries. Her biggest surprise was how few of these high earners were actually wealthy. Though they had a much better opportunity to save and plan for a solid financial future than their middle- or low-income counterparts, they continued to live pay cheque to pay cheque – just at a higher level than the lower-paid women.

12. **Start investing.** Both men and women procrastinate when it comes to investing. The solution is to at least take small steps to move forwards. Do some research, work with small amounts and get started.

13. **It's never too late.** The mistake is thinking it is too late. But that's just an excuse. It's never too late. Get your finances sorted out *now*!

I love this quote that one of my **NLP** practitioners, **Peter Hird**, sent to me:
'Life is great in a Ferrari, yet more enjoyable on a mule ...'.
Make sure you know when to take the mule.

ATTITUDE 8

I'm Certain of My Success

What if you could be as certain about the future as you are about the past? To know for sure that the goals you have set for yourself will happen just as you have planned? The last myth of midlife is that it's too late for you to change. This 8th and final Attitude challenges this by making you 100 per cent certain of the success that lies ahead of you. If you are certain of your success, then it's never too late, is it?

Back to the future

Let's revisit the goals you set for yourself in relation to the first Attitude ('I live my life on purpose'). Whether you've only thought about your goals so far, or you've begun to instigate real change in your life as you've made your way through all the transformational exercises in this book, it's worth remembering that any change leads to more change. Every step you take brings success and learning that will inspire you to make the next move, and the next one, until the momentum of success is well under way.

Remind yourself which areas of your life you chose to work on in Exercise 5 (see page 17), and how you represented those on your Vision Board in Exercise 6. Maybe your Vision Board has pictures of the sort of house you want to live in, where you want to live, the type of partner, job or body you want, or a holiday you'd like to go on. Whatever you have on your Vision Board is perfect. What I want you to do now is to choose the goal which, when you achieve it, would make the biggest difference to you in your life right now. It's important to select only one goal for now, so go for the big one! Once you are familiar with the process, you can use it for your other goals, too.

As always, make sure your goal is a SMART goal (i.e., specific, measurable, achievable, realistic and timed). In my personal view, the two most important factors are 'achievable' and 'realistic'. While you want to really stretch yourself – otherwise it wouldn't be a goal, would it? – at the same time your goal needs to be something that you have a realistic hope of attaining. For example, one of my delegates on my 'Age with Attitude' programme set herself the goal of winning the lottery in the next 6 months. It certainly was a very specific goal, it was measurable because she would either get it or not, it was achievable and it was timed. However, was it realistic? Some may argue that there are no unrealistic goals, only unrealistic time frames. And, yet, the way to set goals is to set goals that are attainable. I used to run marathons. It's certainly *achievable* for me to win the next London Marathon. Yet is it *realistic*? What if I trained every day for the next year? I would certainly improve my time, but would I have improved enough to actually win? It's an interesting question ... Obviously, what is achievable and realistic for you is your decision. I haven't heard yet that my 'Age with Attitude' delegate has won the lottery!

This next exercise is designed to ask you questions to ensure that the goal you have chosen is a totally SMART goal. The more SMART we can make our goal, the more likely it is that we will achieve it so take the time to go through these questions ... it's well worth it. Make sure that you go through it in one go so you can build on your answers.

● **EXERCISE 31**
My goal

STEP 1: WRITE OUT YOUR SMART GOAL BELOW
Make sure you write your goal in the *present* tense, as if you have it *now*. If you write your goals in the future tense, they are more likely to stay in the future. Examples of present-tense goals would be: 'By the end of this year, I am able to hold a conversation in French' or 'In six months' time, I fit into my old jeans'. These are also measurable goals.

....

....

....

....

....

➤

STEP 2: QUESTIONING FOR ACHIEVABLE OUTCOMES

The clearer you can be about what you're aiming for, and the more specific you can be about your goal, the more achievable it becomes. There is a direct relationship between the specificity of your goal and its achievability.

It takes between 25 and 30 minutes to go through the exercise. If possible, it's best to find a partner to do it with. Invite your partner to ask the questions clearly and to coach you through the process as quickly as possible. Ask him or her to write down your answers and give them to you after the exercise. If you can't summon up a partner, you can answer the questions yourself and write down the answers you come up with. It is very important to write the answers down because once you commit the details of your goal to paper, it becomes much more real.

1. **What specifically do you want?**
   (checks that the goal is stated clearly)

2. **For what purpose do you want this goal?**
   (checks that the goal is compelling)

3. **Where are you now in relation to your goal?**
   (checks if you are close to achieving your goal, still some distance away or still at the start of the process. Wherever you are right now is fine.)

4. **What will you see, hear and feel when you have it?** (creates a multi-sensory description that makes the goal more compelling)

➤

5. **How will you know when you have it?**
   (checks that it is measurable)

6. **What do you already have and what do you still need to obtain in order to achieve your outcome?** (checks the resources required to achieve the goal)

7. **What will you gain or lose if you have it?**
   (checks the impact of your goal on other areas of your life)

What did you notice happening to your goal as you went through that process? Most people find that their goal becomes much clearer, and they feel more committed to achieving it. The sensory description (i.e., what will you see, hear and feel when you have it) really attaches you to your goal.

Look at question number 7 in particular. This flushes out what is called 'secondary gain' in NLP. We talked about this concept earlier (see page 23). This question encourages you to think about what you might lose as well as gain when you achieve your goal. For example, losing weight will help you to feel better about yourself, but you are likely to have to stop eating certain foods you like and start to exercise regularly. It's very important that consequences are acknowledged and addressed, because any internal conflict can cause you to give less than 100 per cent commitment to your goal and you may end up compromising on your own success.

> The future is not a gift, it is an achievement.
> Every generation helps make its own future.
> This is the essential challenge of the present
> **Robert F. Kennedy**

Time Line Therapy™

I first came across the technique called Time Line Therapy™ in 1997, when I studied to become a practitioner of NLP, hypnotherapy and Time Line Therapy™. I am now a Certified Master Trainer of Time Line Therapy™ and I use it widely in my practice as a coach and personal-development trainer. Time Line Therapy™ was created by Tad James in 1985. Tad is a well-known American Master Trainer of NLP and one of my teachers.

Time Line Therapy™ is a process that helps us to:

1. **Let go of negative emotions from the past**
   We know that our past experiences and the memories that go with them affect how we approach present-day situations. We often hold on to negative emotions from the past – such as anger towards someone – and we experience that emotion in the present.

2. **Let go of limiting decisions we made in the past**
   We make limiting decisions about ourselves that affect how we view our potential. For example, a young child told by their teacher that they are 'slow' at age 5, may use that statement to unconsciously create a belief about

themselves that they are not intelligent. This may affect their whole lives as they start to filter out all the times they were successful and only pay attention to those times they could have done a better job.

3. **Create our future the way we want it**
    We can also use Time Line Therapy™ to put specific goals into our future in order to be sure that they will happen. It's often said that our destiny is shaped as soon as we make a decision because at that point we start to refocus and take action. Adding goals to your future Time Line works in a similar way.

I'm going to show you how to use Time Line Therapy™ to put the goal you just worked on into your future Time Line to ensure that you achieve it. Before we do that I want to introduce you to the concept of different cultural representations of time as these link to how we store time as individuals as well.

Cultural representations of time

In his book, *Dance of Life*, Edward T. Hall talks about two different cultural representations of time. Neither one is better than the other, and each has its advantages and disadvantages.

- **Monochronic time:** This has its roots in the Industrial Revolution, when the assembly line led to a notion of time as being linear and structured – where one thing happened after another. There is an order and sequence to life that is planned and things happen on time. This model of time is common in Northern European cultures.

● **Polychronic time:** This style enjoys living in the 'now' with spontaneity. It's a much more relaxed style than monochronic time. People in these cultures are typically comfortable with change and they will attempt to keep their options open for as long as possible. They are also typically late for meetings and social events as they have a lack of awareness of time. This model of time is common in Latin America and the Middle East. These countries have a completely different notion of time; their cultures live much more in the 'now' and do many things at once. Their notion of time tends to be something along these lines: 'Time is what is happening now and if I'm late for a meeting it's OK because I was busy and you were doing other things anyway'. Deadlines, if they exist, are to be shifted as there is always 'tomorrow'.

What does this all mean? Bear with me. We'll get to that next.

Eliciting your Time Line

The next step is discover how you store time. Each of us has a way of storing time that means we know the difference between events from the past, now and in the future. Your 'Time Line' is actually how you unconsciously store your memories – or how you know the difference between a memory from the past and a projection of the future. We unconsciously store the memories of everything that ever happened to us; the reason why these memories are not held in our conscious memory is because we would be left with no brain processing power to do anything else!

The language people use often gives clues about how they 'store time'. In fact, the way people speak can often give you a description of what they are literally doing inside their heads. For example, you may have heard people say things like:

- 'I've put it behind me now'
- 'When I look back on that I feel happy'
- 'You've got time on your side'

You may even notice people unconsciously pointing behind them or in some other direction as they speak, referring to a particular point in time. They are actually showing you how they store time.

Going on a journey above your Time Line

In his book *Time Line Therapy™ and the Basis of Personality*, Tad discovered a link between the monochronic and polychronic cultural representations of time, and how we store time as individuals. He goes on to outline how to discover the way in which each of us personally stores time.

So stop for a moment and clear your thoughts. Think about where the past and the future are for you. Begin by considering your memories of things that have happened to you in the past. If I were to say 'Point to your past', where would you point? You will see that your past has a location, and you should take note of where that location is. If you're not sure yet, remember specific events that happened a week, a month, a year, 5 years or 10 years ago. Go with your intuition, as you may just get a feeling about the location. This is something we discover from our unconscious rather than our conscious minds. Trust that your unconscious mind knows where your Time Line is located. Keep going with events in the past until you get a direction and location. Go with what pops into your mind.

Now, consider events in the future. If I were to say 'Point to your future', where would you point? Notice that your future has a different location, and take note of where that is. Whatever you get is perfect. If you're not sure yet, do the same again by thinking about things that will happen in the future – in a week, a month, a year, 5 years or 10 years. Go with your intuition again. Keep going until you get a direction and a location.

You may notice that if your past was behind you, your future is out in front. Or you may notice that both your past and future are out in front of you, running from left to right or right to left – or even up to down. Notice that this arrangement implies a line, or some linear arrangement of your memories.

Your Time Line links to monochronic or polychronic times. The way you view your Time Line is connected to whether you view time as monochronic or polychronic, making you either a 'through time' person or an 'in time' person.

THROUGH TIME

The 'through time' person has their past and future all out in front of them, outside of their body. 'Through time' people don't have to turn their heads to see their Time Lines, which may be organised from right to left, left to right, or up to down. If yours is different, that's OK; just check that it is all out in front of you. If you are a 'through time' person, you will tend to have monochronic tendencies. You are likely to be regularly on time for appointments – even early – and you are organised and plan ahead. On holiday, through time people tend to have the itinerary fixed before they leave, and may become grumpy when others wish to be more spontaneous! They also prefer to deal with issues and move on.

IN TIME

The 'in time' person will tend to code their memories from back to front, where the past is behind them or inside them. They will often turn their bodies to look or point to the past. They are usually less concerned with the past, as it is literally behind them, whereas the 'through time' person has the past out in front and more 'in their face'. The 'in time' person tends to have polychronic tendencies, and if this applies to you, you will like be very spontaneous – choosing to live in the 'now'. You can, however, get so caught up in the now that you are late for appointments.

Living in the now does have some advantages. You can focus and stay focused in even the most chaotic situations – although this may change over a long-term project. 'In time' people prefer to keep their options open and don't like to close down on ideas too quickly. They live a less orderly, more spontaneous, flexible way of life and like to take things as they come. They also tend to look upon 'work time' and 'play time' as being the same – unlike their 'through time' counterparts.

Although these descriptions are generalisations, and you may not find them all existing in you, it is very likely that at least some will be present. You may also find that these descriptions help to explain the behaviour of the people around you. You may now understand why you get on better with some people and less well with others!

● **EXERCISE 32**
Going on a journey above your Time Line

It is a challenge to read this and do the exercise at the same time, so I've made an audio recording, which you can download from my website www.agewithattitude.co.uk. Relax as you listen to my voice guiding you on a journey along your Time Line.

Begin by making yourself comfortable. Close your eyes, knowing that you will be safe and comfortable as you journey above your Time Line. Bring to mind the directions you pointed to and notice that they imply a line. It does not have to be a straight line, but there is an implication of a line there. I would like you to imagine floating up above your Time Line. Float way up in the air, high above your Time Line, and notice it below you. I'd like you to float so high that you're looking down on your Time Line on the entire continuum of your past, present and future.

Now, imagine floating all the way out towards the end of your future Time Line as far as you can, gazing towards the future. Notice the good things that are waiting for you out there. Now, turn around and float back to the present, staying high above your Time Line. Then, float gently into the past along your Time Line. Stay high above it at all times. Notice some of the memories that are stored there. Turn around and float back to now, and come back down into the room. Open your eyes.

How was that? Write down below what you learned from this experience. For example, did you notice specific events in the future and the past? Maybe you noticed a wonderful old memory that you had not thought about for a long time. Did you notice how bright your future is? What is waiting for you out there?

....

....

....

....

....

Now you're used to travelling along your Time Line, we can work together to put your goal into your future Time Line.

Creating your future

Time Line Therapy™ gives us a specific way of creating our future dreams and goals in a simple process that produces results. As you went back into the past, you probably saw memories there, and you know these memories actually happened. What if we could predict that everything we programmed into your future was going to happen, just as everything in the past has already happened? In other words, what if you could be as sure of the future as you are of the past? With Time Line Therapy™ you can decide what is going to happen and when. This process involves using your imagination to create a compelling future that is inspirational. It is important that the goals you put into your future motivate you *now*, because this is what will move you to take action and make your goal a reality.

● **EXERCISE 33**
Putting a goal in your future Time Line

The process below is also available to download in audio format from my website (www.agewithattitude.co.uk).

Get yourself comfortable, relax, close your eyes and follow my voice as it guides you through how to put a goal in your future Time Line. Go back to the goal you selected earlier in this chapter and let's get started.

STEP 1: GET THE LAST STEP
Work out what exactly is the last thing that has to happen for you to be absolutely certain that you have achieved your goal, and write it below. This is your evidence criterion, which goes into your Time Line. For example, if you want to go to Australia for a holiday, the last step may be when you book the tickets, get onto the plane or get off at the other end. My last step might be different from yours – that's OK.

....

....

➤

STEP 2: MAKE AN INTERNAL REPRESENTATION OF YOUR GOAL

Holding the last step in your mind, make it real by turning it into an image in your mind. Notice what you see, hear, feel, smell and touch. Make all those senses come alive. Turn up the brightness of the colours, the sounds and really ramp up those feelings. Make that representation as compelling as you possibly can. Know that it's absolutely inevitable that it will happen.

STEP 3: STEP INTO THE INTERNAL REPRESENTATION OF YOUR GOAL

Imagine you are stepping right into that representation you have just made, and are looking through your own eyes, experiencing everything that is there. Adjust all your senses to get the most 'real' feeling. Enjoy the moment! After enjoying the feeling of achieving your goal, I now need you to step back out of the representation so you can see yourself in it, like looking at yourself in a photograph.

STEP 4: TAKE YOUR INTERNAL REPRESENTATION AND FLOAT ABOVE YOUR TIME LINE

Imagine floating with the representation of your goal above your Time Line as we did before – this time floating above the present.

STEP 5: ENERGISE YOUR REPRESENTATION WITH FOUR BREATHS

This step is taken from the ancient art of Hawaiian Huna,

one of the original arts and sciences of healing and spiritual development. It is a way of bringing your goal alive to the unconscious mind. Breathe in through your nose and out through your mouth four times, and blow all your energy into your internal representation.

STEP 6: FLOAT OUT INTO YOUR FUTURE

Staying above your Time Line, float out into your future — to the point in the future when you want your goal to happen. Allow your unconscious mind to guide you to the 'right' moment. You may just get a feeling that you are there. However you experience this step is perfect.

STEP 7: RELEASE YOUR GOAL INTO YOUR TIME LINE

Imagine letting go of your goal and notice it floating gently down into your future Time Line.

STEP 8: NOTICE THE EVENTS BETWEEN THEN AND NOW RE-EVALUATING THEMSELVES TO SUPPORT YOUR GOAL

Turn around and face 'now'. Notice how all the events between then and now re-evaluate themselves to support you in achieving your goal. Enjoy watching them, knowing that you will absolutely achieve your goal.

STEP 9: FLOAT BACK TO NOW

Float gently back to the present and come back down into the room. Open your eyes.

Now it's time to allow your unconscious mind to deliver your goal to you in ways you expected – and many you did not. If you get 90 per cent of your goal, that's fine, too – maybe a black pair of Jimmy Choos instead of gold! But, if you wanted Jimmy Choos and you got Clarks, thank your unconscious mind and ask again, this time being even more specific. Don't think to yourself: 'I never get what I want', because this puts your unconscious mind in a negative way of thinking.

Achieving your goal is an amazing experience and I wish you many of them!

> To discover more about the other Time Line Therapy™ processes, contact the Time Line Therapy™ Association (www.timelinetherapy.net), who will put you in touch with a Time Line Therapy™ practitioner in your area.

Investing in me

So we are nearing the end of our journey together and I'm wondering just how far you've come. By reading this book, you will have learned that life is a giant self-fulfilling prophecy. Our perception of who we are is very important, as this determines how we perceive the world around us and our role in it. Remember we can never be more than we believe we can be. This is really important.

This book is intended to make you probe deeper into who you really are and what you want for yourself. By now you will be much clearer about who that person is. I hope that your old thoughts and beliefs have been turned on their heads, and that you have begun to understand that who you have told yourself you are may not really be *you* – and that the things you've told yourself you can do are only a faint shadow of what's really possible. Isn't it strange that, without questioning it, we believe our judgements about ourselves and what is possible for us, when even a quick glance on the inside shows us that these judgements are often limited and flawed.

The way to transform our lives is to learn to see ourselves for who we really are, and let our true selves flourish and grow. By discovering ourselves and reaching our own potential, we also give the greatest gift to everyone around us – our children, our families and the world at large. We become a role model for others to follow, as they see in us what is possible for them. To achieve this, we need to learn to suppress our own doubts and excuses so that our true nature can shine through.

So how do you find yourself once and for all? The exercises you've completed have given you an insight into who you are when you are being authentic and true to yourself. Now I'm going to show you how to build on the new you, as you learn more about yourself each time you experiment with something new. Sometimes we feel as though there are two of us – the one who gets caught up in life with no space for herself and who cares too much about what other people think, and the one who knows what it is to feel completely at ease in her skin and unfazed by any problem. We find that easeful part of us in those magical moments when we really connect with someone or something.

Maybe it's no more than a distant, fleeting feeling that makes an appearance once in a blue moon, but it's there – and it shows us that there is a choice, that there is more to our lives when we really allow ourselves to notice. Learning to connect to the real you is vital. It's important to continue the self-reflection that you have undertaken in this book and carry on learning. Whatever you focus on and aim for, make sure that you get feedback about whether it is working or not – if it is, you'll be moving forwards towards your goals. I once asked my teacher how long it would take for me to achieve my goals, and he told me it would take until I got there! I often think about that. The important thing is to keep moving forwards and to learn from anything that doesn't go completely to plan so you can do something differently next time.

One final thing

There is one final thing that will help you to see how far you've come. I've developed a questionnaire that is designed to discover how many of the 8 Attitudes of the Successful Midlife Woman you have managed to adopt as you've progressed through the exercises in this book. Use the results as personal feedback, to assess your own individual development and to work out areas where you still need to make some changes. Have fun, enjoy and learn from your results.

● EXERCISE 34
What's age got to do with it? quiz (Part II)

Choose the answer that is closest to describing you.

● ATTITUDE I: I LIVE MY LIFE ON PURPOSE
I'm clear about where I'm going in my life:
a. I have absolutely no doubt
b. I have a rough idea
c. I still have no clue

➤

● **ATTITUDE 2: I CREATE WHAT I WANT**

My friends would describe me as:

a. Someone who is totally in control of their own destiny

b. Someone who takes responsibility for their life when it suits them

c. Someone who blames other people when things go wrong

● **ATTITUDE 3: I KNOW WHO I AM**

When someone meets me for the first time they would say:

a. I am someone who stands out in the crowd

b. They would find it difficult to remember my name

c. They wouldn't even remember that they had met me!

● **ATTITUDE 4: I AM TRUE TO MYSELF**

I've disappointed other people in order to stay true to who I am:

a. Often

b. Very rarely

c. Never ... that's far too scary!

● **ATTITUDE 5: I AM GOOD ENOUGH**

When you really want something or someone, do you:

a. Go after it (or them) until you are successful?

b. Give up when the going gets tough?

c. Never leave the starting blocks?

➤

● ATTITUDE 6: I LIKE MYSELF
When you look in the mirror, what do you say to yourself (honestly ...)?:

a. Wow!

b. Getting there slowly

c. I avoid looking at all costs!

● ATTITUDE 7: I TAKE TIME FOR ME
When your best friend calls and asks you to go to a spa as a special treat, do you:

a. Find a way of going along whatever it takes?

b. Think about it, then make up an excuse?

c. Don't even call them back?

● ATTITUDE 8: I AM CERTAIN OF MY SUCCESS
When was the last time you achieved something you were going for?

a. Within the last 6 months

b. It has happened but you can't really remember when

c. I never get what I want!

Add up the number of times you chose each letter, and then read below what your results tell you about your progress so far:

MOSTLY As: Congratulations! You are well on the way to living the 8 Attitudes of the Successful Midlife Woman. Well done. You are someone who is truly authentic and knows where she's going. You're not afraid to take a few risks along the way and learn from your experiences. You are happy and confident in your own skin. You enjoy the challenge of going after what you want and you are resilient when things don't always go to plan. You are enjoying your midlife, as it gives you lots of new opportunities and you feel totally liberated. Good luck for the future and remember that you are good enough to achieve anything you set your mind to, no matter what is going on around you.

MOSTLY Bs: You've started your journey but there's still a way to go before you are living the 8 Attitudes of the Successful Midlife Woman.

Your biggest challenge is keeping focused on what you want. You tend to get distracted by people and problems that 'appear' to get in your way. Although you know what you'd like to change, you do not yet totally believe that it's possible – and that you can do it. You tend to start off enthusiastically, but don't have the discipline needed to follow through. When the going gets tough you tend to make excuses about why you can't make progress or hide behind those who can. You tend to spend your time day dreaming about what you'd like in your life; however, unless you're prepared to take action, nothing will change. Remember this phrase: if you always do what you've always done, you'll always get what you've always got! Reread Attitudes 1, 2, 5 and 6, and really go for it this time. Know that you can absolutely have what you want if you're prepared to stand out in the crowd!

➤

MOSTLY Cs: You are still in the starting blocks wondering whether to move or not. The 8 Attitudes of the Successful Midlife Woman can be yours if you're prepared to take a small step forwards.

You picked up this book so I know you want to make some changes in your life. This is a real moment of truth for you when you need to decide just how much you want to make these changes. If you really do want things to be different for you, let's stop the excuses and get started. You are missing out on so many of life's opportunities as you let most of them pass you by. Make sure you have a goal, even if it's a small one, and break it down into small steps. Then start to take action at a pace at which you feel comfortable. Each small step will take you forwards, and before too long you'll be surprised at how much you've achieved. Reread the whole book, take a deep breath and take a small step towards change. If you do that every day, you'll soon catch the others up!

My last word

How did you get on with the questionnaire? Did you get any surprises? We get out of life what we put in, so it's time to start putting in. And, if as a result of reading this book, you become really successful and get exactly what you want, don't blame me!

As a change-management consultant I learned about a general model of change that applies to individuals, groups and organisations. It was first developed by Richard Beckhard, a change-management consultant. He said that for change to occur, there needs to be sufficient motivational energy in the system under review. To discover if that energy is likely to be present, he came up with the 'change equation'.

It helps to answer these two questions, which may well be on your mind right now:

1. Should I be attempting to change things?
2. What do I need to do to make the chances of change occurring in my life more likely?

He said that change will occur if (stay calm and breathe ...!):

$$(V \times D \times S) > F$$

This is where:

V = Your vision for the future or your goals
D = Your dissatisfaction with your current life
S = Knowing how to take the 'first practical steps'
F = Your level of fear of doing something different

To put it in plain English, if you have compelling goals for the future, you are unhappy with your life and you are clear about what to do to take the initial steps forwards, this will be enough to overcome any fear of change you experience. And those goals, dissatisfaction and knowledge need to be *strong*.

If you are still not prepared to make a change, it means that one of those elements (goals, dissatisfaction and/or knowledge of first steps) is not yet strong enough. If that is the case for you, ask yourself which element you need to do some more work on. What is the 'tipping point' that will move you forwards? Do you need a more compelling goal? Is your level of dissatisfaction with your current life not bad enough yet? Or are you still unsure about the first step to take? Once all these are clear, you will move forwards – I promise you that. Go back to your Vision Board and make sure that you use it to inspire you every day. It's designed to give you energy and momentum for the future.

I've enjoyed being on this journey with you and I really hope that I've inspired you to live all of the 8 Attitudes of the Successful Midlife Woman. The only way to truly change is from the inside out and the Attitudes enable you to do just that. The Attitudes also empower us to leave a legacy to our children and families about faith and hope for the future, because they help us to be true to ourselves and to believe in who we are. Midlife is about beginnings not endings, and I wish you many new beginnings. Let my words stay with you as you enjoy your journey. Here's to your wellbeing, health and a deeper joy in living your life.

What Is NLP?

Unlike other approaches that tell you *what* you need to do, NLP, or 'neurolinguistic programming', is a *how-to* technique. It tells and shows you how to be what you want to be, have what you want to have, and do what you want to do. And that's an intoxicating combination. This means that it is possible to have the personal success you want – now!

For most people, things happen and they react instinctively. NLP offers a better way. It gives you tools to enable you to react differently by choice, to be more aware of your thoughts, feelings and behaviour. You are then ready to take responsibility for your results in all areas of your life.

NLP provides a set of tools and techniques to help you deal with unhelpful patterns of thought and behaviours that may be holding you back. Let's look at each part of NLP in turn and I'll explain what it's all about.

Neuro

'Neuro' is all about what we think.

'Neuro' literally means 'what goes on inside our heads'. We have over 60,000 thoughts a day. These form our internal world of pictures, sounds and feelings. It is the conversations, dialogues or arguments we have with ourselves in our thinking process that drive how we feel, our mood and ultimately how we respond to events. In NLP terms, these are called our 'internal representations'.

The critical point to realise is that we can control our thoughts. This is very important because how we feel, how we behave and ultimately the results we get are driven by combinations of these internal representations, which form our repeating patterns or habits. We run these patterns or habits over and over again, unless they are interrupted or redirected. Sometimes these patterns serve us well, but often they sabotage our potential success. For example, if you open your curtains on a miserable rainy day you may feel lousy, and this will drive how your day goes for you. Alternatively, you can open the curtains and think to yourself 'It's a brilliantly rainy day today!' and go off and have fun. Or, let's look at what happens when you are getting ready to go on a date with a potential new partner. If you are excited and focused on the evening going well, this will impact positively on how you feel – and will make it much more likely that the evening will be a success. By contrast, if you go out believing the date will be a disaster like the last date you went on, or that it won't lead to anything as you're destined to be alone, chances are the evening will be a complete failure. The trick is to ensure that the 60,000 thoughts you have every day are good ones!

Linguistic

'Linguistic' is all about what we say, both verbally and non-verbally.

Language determines how we communicate with other

people and ourselves. It is how we label what we believe about ourselves, and our role in the world. Empowering language generates empowered behaviour. Likewise, negative language, such as excuses, is the result of disempowering thoughts and often occurs without our realising it. It is negative language that limits our choices.

However, it is not only the words we use that have this effect; it is estimated that 93 per cent of communication is non-verbal. This means that how you say what you say (intonation, volume, speed, etc.) carries five times more information than the words spoken. And how you use your body (gestures, facial expressions, posture) is even more influential. As our thoughts and feelings literally 'leak' out of us through our bodies, consider what yours says about you. Does your body language portray low self-esteem, or someone who has confidence and knows what they want?

Programming

'Programming' is all about what we do.

We are all running programmes in our minds, all of the time. These programmes drive the way we behave, our performance and ultimately our results. A phobia is a good example of this type of programming. For example, if someone has a fear of flying, when they fly their nervous system produces a strong physical response (sweaty palms, fast breathing, panic, etc.). The brain learns quickly and, thereafter, every time the person is presented with the same stimulus, their body knows to have the same response. Often, as with phobias, you run strategies that do not serve you well. In fact, they may even sabotage you. NLP teaches us how to change these ineffective and possibly even destructive strategies or programmes forever.

Applications of NLP

NLP shows how what we say, think and do interplay and affect our body and behaviour, and ultimately impact on how successful we are.

With NLP you can learn how to be in charge of your mental and physical state, create the perfect relationship, achieve success in your career, make more money, increase your motivation, boost your confidence and communicate effectively to produce the kind of results you want. One of the best things about NLP is that it has been designed to be learned easily and it can be applied in any professional or personal situation. NLP can help you to:

- lift low self-esteem
- feel happier
- banish anxiety from your life
- get rid of bad habits
- lose weight and keep it off
- get out of debt
- work out what you want in life
- find the perfect partner or career
- communicate better
- learn faster
- reach peak performance in sport
- get messages across effectively

This book will have helped you to achieve many, or even all, of these things. Remember, age is just a number – and change is in your hands. It's up to you to make your life the way you want it to be, and anything you want is possible. The most exciting and empowering stage of your life is only just beginning!

Going Further

Taking steps to create and achieve goals is a brave and powerful step, and this book has provided you with all of the tools you need to do just that. The 8 Attitudes of the Successful Midlife Woman are designed to get you where you want to be. You may, however, wish to explore other development opportunities in more detail, and you'll find some information below, which will help you on whatever path you choose to take. If you wish to develop yourself or your company further by training personally with me, this is what we provide:

The Change Corporation

Corporate programmes

We use NLP in our work to deliver performance improvement for our clients. We offer bespoke in-house programmes to meet your specific requirements in the areas of change management, leadership, team development and well-being. Our blue-chip clients include Carl Zeiss, DHL,

Nokia, PricewaterhouseCoopers, Kent County Council and Durham University MBA programme.

NLP (based) programmes

- *Age with Attitude*™ is our new and unique programme that complements this book. After years of prioritising husbands and families, many women want more out of their lives as they approach midlife. The urge to refocus and find personal fulfilment is overwhelming. This is a unique personal development programme for midlife women, and it's the first of its kind. It is a 10-day programme spread across four events, with coaching and assistance in between each event to help keep you on track to achieve your goals. It is a journey on which you work with other like-minded women who will support and inspire you to create the changes you want to make in your life.

- *Re-Vitalise Your Life: The Method Part I* is designed for people who want to get energy and focus back into their lives. We guide you through our unique method of the 7 Fs: Focus, Feeling, Food, Fitness, Flexibility, Feedback and Future.

- *Powerful Presentations* is a programme that uses NLP to build your confidence and beliefs as a presenter. Many people are more scared of speaking in public than almost anything else. Powerful Presentations teaches you how to present with charisma in any situation and get the results you want.

- *7-Day Fast Track NLP Practitioner, Practitioner of Time Line Therapy*™ *and Practitioner of Hypnotherapy*: You will learn how to use NLP techniques to transform your own life and help others. Our Practitioner programme allows you to become a Certified Practitioner of NLP in 7 days, saving you 13 days of traditional classroom time. We do this by utilising pre-study CDs that you will then be able to use long after the training has finished as a useful refresher. You will also study to become a Practitioner of Time Line Therapy™ and a Practitioner of Hypnosis.

- *14-Day Fast Track NLP Master Practitioner, Master Practitioner of Time Line Therapy™ and Master Hypnotist*: Our Master Practitioner programme will teach you many advanced techniques to enable you to take your practitioner skills to a mastery level. Everything then comes together at the end of the programme through a breakthrough session where you will coach a client and be coached yourself in a truly transformational experience. You will also have the opportunity to become a Master Practitioner of Time Line Therapy™ and a Master Hypnotist. This programme also has a pre-study component.

- *BreakThrough Coaching* offers a fast-track way of dealing with long-term limiting patterns of behaviour. We work intensively together for one day to resolve a particular issue with follow-up assistance.

- *Free Buddy Service* is designed to 'buddy' our readers with like-minded women to work together to achieve their outcomes. All you have to do is email or call us, and we'll let you know if we have anyone available to work with you. We put you in touch and then it's over to you.

If you would like more information on NLP or the courses available from The Change Corporation, send an email to info@thechangecorporation.com or visit our websites:

- **www.agewithattitude.co.uk**
- **www.thechangecorporation.com**
- **www.lindseyagness.com**

Further Reading

Agness, Lindsey, *Change Your Life with NLP* (Pearson, 2008)

Bandler, Richard & Grinder, J., *Reframing: NLP and the Transformation of Meaning* (Real People Press, 1982)

Chopra, Deepak, *Ageless Body, Timeless Mind* (Harmony Books, 1993)

Csikszentmihalyi, Mihaly, *Flow: The Psychology of Optimum Experience* (Harper, 2008)

Dylan, Peggy, *Femme Vital* (not yet published)

Frankel, Lois P., *Nice Girls Don't Get Rich: 75 Avoidable Mistakes Women Make with Money* (Warner Books, 2005)

Frankl, Victor E., *Man's Search for Meaning* (Ebury, 2004)

Hall, Edward T., *Dance of Life: The Other Dimension of Time* (Anchor, 1984)

Hill, Napoleon, *Think and Grow Rich* (Aventine Press, 1937; reprinted 2004)

James, Tad & Woodsmall Wyatt, *Time Line Therapy*™ *and the Basis of Personality* (Meta Publishers, 1988)

Korzybski, Alfred, *Science and Sanity* (Institute of General Semantics, 1933)

Maltz Max, *Psycho-Cybernetics* (Prentice Hall, 1960)

Northrup, Christiane, *The Secret Pleasures of Menopause* (Hay House, 2008)

Pert, Candace B., *Everything You Need to Know to Feel Good About Yourself* (Hay House, 2006)

Pert, Candace B., *Molecules of Emotion* (Scribner, 1997)

Spur, Dr Pam, *You & Him: Getting to the Heart of Your Relationship Potential* (Thorsons, 2000)

Stanley, Thomas J., *The Millionaire Mind* (Bantam Press, 2002)

Stanny, Barbara, *Secrets of Six-Figure Women: Surprising Strategies To Up Your Earnings and Change Your Life* (Harper Collins, 2002)

ACKNOWLEDGEMENTS

To my amazing children, Sophie and Oliver, who inspire me each day and give me space to create my work.

To my mother, who is always there.

To Jonny, my nurturer.

To my sister, who makes it all work while I write.

To my girl-friends. You know who you are. Thank you for the inspiration for this book.

To Pam, Jenna and Rebecca for your relentless hard work on my behalf.

Finally, to my agent Jane Graham Maw and the team at Rodale, especially Liz Gough and Lorraine Green. Thank you for making this dream a reality.

- I would also like to thank Peggy Dylan, Tad James, Becca Levy, Nikki Owen, Dr Candace Pert and Henry Whitfield for permission to reference their work.

- The exercise on pp160-63 is adapted with permission from The Self-Esteem Gift Box process, developed by Nikki Owen, creator of the seminar An Audience with Charisma.

- Section entitled 'What is NLP?', pp265–268: reproduced with permission from *Change Your Life with NLP* by Lindsey Agness, published by Pearson Education Ltd, 2008.

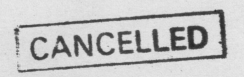